MW00965842

Escott Reid

Escott Reid

DIPLOMAT AND SCHOLAR

Edited by
Greg Donaghy and
Stéphane Roussel

MCGILL-QUEEN'S UNIVERSITY PRESS
MONTREAL & KINGSTON • LONDON • ITHACA

© McGill-Queen's University Press 2004
ISBN 0-7735-2713-3

Legal deposit fourth quarter 2004
Bibliothèque nationale du Québec

Printed in Canada on acid-free paper that is 100% ancient forest free (100% post-consumer recycled), processed chlorine free.

This book has been published with the help of grants from the Canadian Federation for the Humanities and Social Sciences, through the Aid to Scholarly Publications Programme, using funds provided by the Social Sciences and Humanities Research Council of Canada, and from Glendon College, York University.

McGill-Queen's University Press acknowledges the support of the Canada Council for the Arts for our publishing program. We also acknowledge the financial support of the Government of Canada through the Book Publishing Industry Development Program (BPIDP) for our publishing activities.

Title page photo: Escott Reid, 1963 (Frost Library Archives)

LIBRARY AND ARCHIVES CANADA CATALOGUING IN PUBLICATION

Escott Reid : diplomat and scholar / edited by Greg Donaghy and Stéphane Roussel.
Includes bibliographical references and index.
ISBN 0-7735-2713-3
1. Reid, Escott.   2. Canada – Foreign relations – 1918–1945.   3. Canada – Foreign relations – 1945–   4. Diplomats – Canada – Biography.
5. Intellectuals – Canada – Biography.   6. World Bank – Officials and employees – Biography.   7. Glendon College – Officials and employees – Biography.   I. Donaghy, Greg   II. Roussel, Stéphane, 1964–
FC601.R44E83 2004   327.71'0092   C2004-903146-5

Set in 10.5/13.5 Electra and Frutiger Condensed. Book design and typesetting by zijn digital.

POUR CHANTAL
— S.R.

FOR MARY
— G.D.

Contents

Foreword

Canada Looks Ahead: Escott Reid and Lester B. Pearson

GEOFFREY A.H. PEARSON

Near the village of Wakefield, Quebec, lie the graves of four architects of post-war Canadian foreign policy – Escott Reid, L.B. Pearson, Norman Robertson, and Hume Wrong. That they lie side by side is no accident – all had summer properties in the area and chose their final resting places quite deliberately. The cemetery is twenty minutes or so by road from the East Block of the Parliament Buildings where they had spent much of their working lives, and the simple head stones bespeak the modesty and the clarity which those lives represented. While Pearson rose later to public prominence and leadership, at the time the site was chosen they did not "seek for a monument" but rather for a memory of the kind of pioneering country – logging and milling were local industries – they had sought to bring to maturity on the stage of world diplomacy.

They were both friends and rivals. Pearson and Wrong had worked together before the war in London and Geneva, and had common ties to the Department of History at the University of Toronto. Wrong followed Pearson to Washington where he, too, became a friend of Dean Acheson. They played bad golf together. Their wives were close friends. Robertson and Reid arrived later on the Ottawa scene, and while the Robertson family too became Pearson family friends, the two men followed different paths to the top of the Department of External Affairs and shared few common interests outside the East Block – Robertson, the son of a classics professor, was happiest in his library or at the bridge table, while Pearson preferred the company of journalists and tennis players.

Reid joined the Department some years later than the others, but rapidly found himself at the centre of policy-making over the creation of the United Nations (UN) in 1945 and of the North Atlantic Treaty Organization (NATO) in 1948. He and Pearson were both sons of the manse and, unlike Robertson and Wrong, the sons of professors, they tended to advocate rather than instruct, although they rarely resorted to the language of the gospels and they arrived at their views from different premises – Pearson from his experience of war and the failure of the League, Reid from his faith in social democracy. However, Pearson did not share what he called in his memoirs the "single-minded intensity" of Reid. His experience as a diplomat taught him the virtues of patience and timing.

Both men had two main goals in mind – creating a "new world order" and finding a major role for Canada in such a creation ("a nation with a mission" as Reid puts it in his memoirs.) The aim was collective security, and by this they meant economic and social as well as military security. Thus the UN Charter must contain provisions for economic development and the protection of human rights as well as military co-operation, and the North Atlantic Treaty had to go beyond collective defence to include what Pearson called the vision of an Atlantic Community. Indeed, he and Reid were world federalists. If achieving this was not possible soon or on a global scale, then let the Western democracies show the way.

Reid is perhaps best known as the "Envoy to Nehru." He was fortunate to go to New Delhi when he did, in 1952, two years after the Colombo plan had been agreed and when India appeared to be a key prize in the developing Cold War. Reid found in Indian Prime Minister Jawaharlal Nehru a leader who represented his own deepest beliefs – social democracy, anti-colonialism, and minority rights. He was, indeed, "captivated by India," and this led him to attach greater importance to India's place in Cold War politics than Ottawa was prepared to accept, especially over Indochina policy and during the Suez crisis. This was partly a matter of personality. Inhabitants of foreign offices are wary of emotion, especially enthusiasm. Reid's energy and ability found their outlet in a cascade of messages to the department, which even L. B. Pearson found difficult to absorb, whether or not he agreed with the contents. He too was attracted by Nehru and India (his prescription for dealing with the out-spoken Indian politician and diplomat Krishna Menon was "tea and sympathy").

But Pearson had to negotiate with the United States secretary of state, John Foster Dulles, as well, and in the end there was little doubt where the balance of policy had to be struck.

In his reflections on Lester B. Pearson in his memoirs, Reid speaks of "the most difficult task which faces any Canadian government" – that of "doing our utmost to dissuade the US from pursuing an unwise policy in its foreign relations." Pearson did this, he writes, by working with the UN, NATO, and the Commonwealth. Reid was no doubt thinking of US relations with China in the 1950s, of Vietnam, and, more generally, of Cold War crusading. It is true that in a world of nuclear weapons, the use of which could lead to an attack on North America, Canada has a vital interest in means to control tensions between the US and potential enemies, and therefore to enlist the support of friends and allies. But Canada is also more dependent than others on defence and trade relations with the US, thus limiting our capacity to "dissuade." Pearson understood this well, just as he sympathised with Escott Reid's "singledminded" search for a new world order.

Acknowledgments

This book would not have been possible without the active support of a large number of individuals and organizations. The Department of Foreign Affairs and International Trade encouraged the editors to pursue this project from an early date and generously helped fund a workshop for the contributors. The workshop was only made possible by additional grants from Glendon College, the Canadian Institute of International Affairs, and the Groupe d'étude et de recherche sur la sécurite internationale.

The editors have also received substantial support and encouragement from a diverse group of people interested in Escott Reid's career. Gratefully, we would like the acknowledge the help of Nicolas-Dominic Audet, Gaston Barban, Richard Bingham, Christopher Cook, Tom Delworth, Anne-Marie Durocher, Yves Frenette, Mary Halloran, John Hilliker, Norman Hillmer, Michiel Horn, Guy Larocque, Louis-Blaise Dumais-Lévesque, Barbara McDougall, Geoffrey Pearson, Patrick Reid, Tim Reid, Françoise Reme, Michelle Rossi, Michael Stevenson, and Marie Josée Therrien. We would especially like to acknowledge the help and encouragement of Kenneth MacRoberts, principal of Glendon College, who strongly supported this project from its inception. Without his continued assistance, the project would not have been possible.

Finally, we would like to thank our wives and children for tolerating our absences – both figurative and literal – while we worked on this project.

Institute of Pacific Relations Conference at Banff, Alberta, in 1933. Reid is seated in the first row, third from the left (NAC/PA-202323)

Escott Reid, Ottawa, August 1947 (Foreign Affairs Canada)

Escott Reid and the secretary of state for external affairs, Lester B. Pearson, examine a globe before heading to the Commonwealth Foreign Ministers' Meeting in Colombo, Sri Lanka, December 1949 (NAC/PA-121700)

Escott Reid, chairman of the United Nations committee on procedures and organization, checking dictation with stenographer Ruth Hyde, Lake Placid, September 1947 (F. Royal/W. Doucette/NAC/PA-128998)

सत्यमेव जयते

Escott Reid and Indian Prime Minister Jawaharlal Nehru sign the Canada-India Reactor Agreement in New Delhi on 28 April 1956 (Government of India/NAC/PA-212090)

Escott Reid chats with Indian politician Krishna Menon at the airport in New Delhi, February 1957 (NAC/PA-212088)

Escott Reid presents his credentials to Theodor Heuss, president of the Federal Republic of Germany, at Bonn in the spring of 1958 (NAC/e002107726)

Escott Reid, director of the World Bank's South Asia and Middle East Department, greets the president of Pakistan, General Muhammad Ayub Khan, in Karachi on 18 February 1960 (NAC/e002107727)

Prime Minister Lester B. Pearson addresses the audience at the opening of Glendon College in September 1966, while Escott Reid (seated) looks on (NAC/e002107729)

A contemporary view of the residences of Glendon College

Escott Reid (left) and the Hon. Leslie Frost at the opening of the Frost Library, Glendon College, 9 October 1963

Escott Reid

Introduction

Escott Reid: A Liberal Idealist in a Hard-Power World

GREG DONAGHY AND STÉPHANE ROUSSEL

Students of post-war Canadian diplomacy ought to be well-acquainted with Escott Reid. Though Reid spent much of his career cloistered behind the opaque doors of the Ottawa bureaucracy, where he was often overshadowed by more luminous contemporaries such as Lester B. Pearson or Norman Robertson, he worked very hard in retirement to favourably shape the historical record. His accounts of the early years of the United Nations (UN), the birth of the North Atlantic Treaty Organization (NATO), and Indo-Canadian relations in the mid-1950s have done much to establish his reputation as a far-sighted idealist.[1] Part history, part memoir, each of Reid's studies, while brutally honest and forthright, was prepared with a careful eye on his place in history. "Reid is the only one I know," a prominent Canadian historian once quipped, "to edit his papers before donating them to the National Archives."[2]

Despite the books and articles, as well as the innumerable and detailed memoranda and despatches that he left behind in the dusty files of the Department of External Affairs, historians have not treated Reid as seriously as he deserves. Often arrogant and given to excess, Reid is easy to dislike and easy to caricature. Typecast as a slightly naive liberal idealist in a hard-power world, Reid is often acknowledged as the prophetic voice in post-war Canadian diplomacy but only to emphasize the sterling pragmatism of his more solidly grounded contemporaries.[3] Few scholars have tried to engage Reid and his diplomatic and academic careers on his terms, using the documentary record to understand his idealism, its limits, and how he sought to transform the rhetoric into action.

Admittedly, coming to terms with Reid is not easy. His considerable intelligence, striking good looks, and widespread personal connections lent real weight to his views. But the impact of his opinions was frequently weakened by the unshakable arrogance with which he delivered them. This was complicated by Reid's tendency to drive himself into emotional bouts of exhaustion and depression. It is hardly surprising that contemporary observers often found it hard to characterize him and difficult to assess his significance. In December 1948, for example, South Africa's roving ambassador Charles te Water dismissed Reid, then acting undersecretary of state for external affairs, as "not very important."[4] In contrast, observers at the United States embassy in Ottawa concluded four years later that Reid exerted "considerable influence" over Canada's approach to the UN, the Far East, and the Korean War.[5]

It is perhaps even harder for scholars today to measure Reid's worth. While it is certainly true that he played a significant role in the creation of the UN and NATO, it is not always possible to define his precise contribution – a difficulty compounded by his failure to reach the highest levels in the Department of External Affairs. Moreover, scholars focusing on individuals as policy-makers are apt to fall prey to a common methodological trap and overestimate their subject's role and responsibilities. Still, given the amount of material written by and about Reid, and its particular perspective, it seemed worthwhile to invite a handful of scholars to take on these challenges and mine the documentary record to critically explore the tension between Reid's idealism and the real world in which he operated. This book, which offers a sustained but largely sympathetic critique of Reid's career as diplomat, international civil servant, and academic, is the result.

For Jack Granatstein – whose pioneering study *The Ottawa Men: The Civil Service Mandarins* was one of the first efforts to tackle Reid on his own ground – Reid remains very much defined by his intelligent radicalism and boundless energy. Born in January 1905, as the reformist social gospel movement swept over the Anglican manse where he grew up, Reid was a natural rebel, always "in full battle against conventional wisdom." His socialism and enthusiasm for hard work emerged early on and shaped his progress through the University of Toronto and Oxford University. After working briefly on a Ph.D., Reid joined the new Canadian Institute of International Affairs (CIIA) as its national secretary in 1932. Armed with a radical critique of Canadian foreign policy that reflected his generation's revulsion at the losses of the First World War, Reid soon found himself and his ideas at odds with the conservative businessmen who had founded the CIIA. Stubbornly clinging to principle, Reid was eventually overwhelmed by his enthusiasm, and his position at the CIIA became untenable. He was forced to seek refuge in the Department of External Affairs, which he joined in December 1938. He was posted immediately to Washington as second secretary.

The Department of External Affairs in the late 1930s was still a relatively cosy and tolerant place to work. The under-secretary, O.D. Skelton, was once viewed as a progressive himself, and while he learned to temper his views to suit those of his political masters, he welcomed debate and diversity of opinion among his juniors. Reid fit in well. Indeed, when the Royal Canadian Mounted Police (RCMP) reported that Reid had received a Communist flyer from Moscow in August 1940, Skelton quickly leapt to his defence. "Mr. Reid," he wrote the police commissioner, "is one of the most valuable members of our Service and a man in whom we have complete confidence."[6]

Reid's diplomatic career blossomed as the Second World War stretched the capacity of Canada's small foreign service. After returning to Ottawa in May 1941 to work in the American and Far Eastern Division, he was promoted to first secretary in March 1944. A year later, in April 1945, he was promoted again, to counsellor at the Canadian High Commission in London. He served on Canada's delegation to the founding conference of the UN in San Francisco and later in London as Pearson's deputy on the executive committee of the UN preparatory commission for the first General Assembly.

But as Hector Mackenzie makes clear in chapter 2, the successful diplomat who headed out for the UN in the spring of 1945 was not the same man whose excessive radicalism had cost him his job with the CIIA. The years in Ottawa and Washington had matured Reid. While a passionate and progressive idealism still drove his work – giving rise to bouts of optimism as he contemplated the possibilities of a new world order and outrage at the shortsighted pragmatism of Canada's timid prime minister, William Lyon Mackenzie King – he more often directed his energies to issues where he could make a practical difference. He worked hard, for example, clarifying draft resolutions, the wording of the UN

Charter, and the UN's rules of procedures, seeking transparent language that would both inspire and reflect the democratic aspirations of the world's people. Indeed, perhaps he worked too hard, suffering the first of several bouts of exhaustion and depression that would mark, and ultimately hamper, his career. Nevertheless, Reid's efforts to translate his liberal vision for the new UN into a concrete reality did not go unrewarded. In April 1947 he was again promoted, becoming the assistant under-secretary responsible for much of the Department's core foreign policy functions.

The creative tension between Reid's idealism and his realism is also the principal theme in the essay contributed by David Haglund and Stéphane Roussel. These two political scientists explore the complex of ideas that prompted Reid to become one of the first statesmen of the early Cold War to suggest that the West respond to the growing antagonism of the Soviet Union with a North Atlantic alliance that would unite Europe and North America. They argue that in Reid's view the alliance was intended to provide Canada with a "counterweight" to the powerful United States – a stroke of *realpolitik* worthy of Bismarck – while simultaneously creating the nucleus for a genuine transnational North Atlantic community – an ideal worthy of Kant. Haglund and Roussel eventually develop a conceptual model capable of reconciling the idealist with the realist but not before they take their analysis a step further, weighing the long-term value of Reid's ideas. Ironically, it is Reid's success in translating the realist notion of a balance of power/counterweight into action and its enduring influence on how Canadian policy-makers see their world that figures most prominently in their discussion.

Reid's work on the NATO negotiations earned him a promotion to deputy under-secretary in September 1948. But Pearson's confidence in Reid was never unqualified. "Escott is as busy and active and useful as ever but emotionally unstable, and I sometimes get worried about him," the minister wrote on Reid's return from the UN General Assembly in the fall of 1947. "He is showing signs the last two or three weeks of mental fatigue. This always means for him a certain irrationality of conduct and an intolerance of viewpoint."[7] Reid's alarming tendency to drive himself to exhaustion in pursuit of his ideals was only too apparent during the lengthy period of recurring crises that followed the outbreak of the Korean War in June 1950. By the spring of 1951 he was temporarily sidelined, responsible for overseeing an inconclusive foreign policy review and passed over again for promotion to under-secretary, the most senior job in the Canadian foreign service. In 1952 he accepted a post as high commissioner to India.

Like the contributions of both Mackenzie and Haglund and Roussel, Greg Donaghy's chapter on Reid in India places much emphasis on Reid's realism and his pragmatic diplomacy. Though attracted to democratic India by its pivotal importance in the Asian Cold War and by Nehru's moral authority, Reid arrived in New Delhi in the spring of 1952 more determined than ever to restrain his enthusiasms and play the careful diplomat. Between 1952 and 1955, as Donaghy argues, he did this with some success. Though he rarely won complete victories, Reid's tightly argued despatches, which hinted at a deeper passion, delighted Pearson and ensured that New Delhi continued to figure prominently in Canadian calculations about Asia. Trouble loomed, however, when Reid's hopes for an Indo-Canadian entente encountered the realities of war in Vietnam and the Middle East. As India and Canada went their separate ways, Reid's emotions got the better of him, with his erratic behaviour during the Suez Crisis irreparably damaging his prospects in Ottawa.

Reid left India shortly after the Suez Crisis, reluctantly becoming ambassador to West Germany, an important Canadian ally in NATO. Drawn partly by the prospect of working at the very centre of the North Atlantic community that he had advocated in the late 1940s, he was soon disillusioned. Life in Bonn was dull and drab, and NATO's moment had long passed, replaced by the monotony of assisting Canadian military sales to Germany. Although Reid impressed the new Conservative prime minister, John G. Diefenbaker, who visited Bonn in 1958, with his administrative expertise and his grasp of world affairs, his lengthy unsolicited missives to the Prime Minister's Office went largely unread and unacknowledged. In 1962, convinced that he would never reach the highest ranks of the foreign service – ambassador in Washington, high commissioner in London, or under-secretary in Ottawa – Reid left the Department of External Affairs.

Not surprisingly, he sought a field where his progressive views might flourish. At the invitation of the legendary head of the World Bank, Eugene Black, he joined the International Bank for Reconstruction and Development (IBRD) in 1962, and eventually became head of the South Asia and Middle East Department. Reid arrived in Washington at an opportune moment, when both the Bank and India were anxious to change established patterns of aid. In his essay on Reid at the World Bank, Bruce Muirhead explores the former diplomat's efforts to convince the IBRD to shed its Anglo-American perspective and embrace a philosophy of development that stressed progress at the grassroots level. Ever the pragmatist, Reid also encouraged India to embrace the discipline of the market and urged the World Bank to exert direct control over its projects in India.

Though Reid revelled in challenging accepted practices, he grew tired of fighting the World Bank's deeply conservative bureaucracy. More important, he found himself estranged from Black's successor, the prickly and overbearing George Woods. In 1965, after searching in vain for a position with the federal government in Ottawa, he left the IBRD to become the first head of York University's Glendon College. Reid relished the challenge of creating a small, fully bilingual, fully residential, liberal arts college. For Reid, as Alyson King suggests in the concluding chapter of this book, Glendon College offered the opportunity to construct a university college that emphasized the progressive public service values that had characterized his own career in Ottawa and Washington.

This was no easy challenge and many of his friends worried that Reid was seeking another impossible ideal. The rapid growth of Ontario's system of post-secondary education in the 1960s made it difficult to find the funding and resources he needed. Moreover, the new generation of affluent and rebellious students that appeared on campus in the mid-1960s had its own, different agenda. But Reid fought hard for his vision, undeterred by stingy administrators, balky faculty, or striking students. And, for once, Reid's single-minded pursuit of his idealistic objective became a strength rather than a weakness.

The papers in this collection challenge those scholars who would dismiss Reid as an impractical and ineffectual idealist. As this volume makes clear, Reid's approach to policy-making was more sophisticated than that and his idealism was often tempered by an astute grasp of the competing interests of a host of national and bureaucratic powers. Indeed, it was the creative tension generated by these two contradictory impulses – the idealistic and the realistic – that inspired and defined Reid's contribution to public policy in Canada and abroad.

NOTES

1 Escott Reid, *On Duty: A Canadian at the Making of the United Nations, 1945–1949* (Toronto: University of Toronto Press, 1983); *Time of Fear and Hope: The Making of the North Atlantic Treaty, 1947–1949* (Toronto: University of Toronto Press, 1977); *Envoy to Nehru* (Toronto: Oxford University Press, 1981). Reid also wrote a study of his activities during the Suez Crisis, *Hungary and Suez 1956: A View from New Delhi* (Oakville, Ont.: Mosaic Press, 1986), as well as a more conventional memoir, *Radical Mandarin: The Memoirs of Escott Reid* (Toronto: University of Toronto Press, 1989).

2 Bruce Muirhead to Greg Donaghy, 8 September 2001.

3 This theme is prominent in the main works on Reid. See especially, J.L. Granatstein, *The Ottawa Men: The Civil Service Mandarins, 1935–1957* (Toronto: Oxford University Press, 1982), chapter 8; Shelagh D. Grant, "Escott Meredith Reid: The Makings of a Radical Diplomat," *Queen's Quarterly* 91/3 (Autumn 1984), 594–611; and Alice K. Young, "Escott Reid as Cold Warrior?: A Canadian Diplomat's Reflections on the Soviet Union," in J.L. Black and Norman Hillmer, eds., *Nearly Neighbours. Canada and the Soviet Union: From Cold War to Détente and Beyond* (Kingston: R.P. Frye, 1989), 29–41; Geoffrey Pearson, "Remembering Escott Reid," *Behind the Headlines* 57, no. 1 (Fall 1999); and Benjamin Rogers et al, "Escott Reid: Issues and Causes," *Behind the Headlines* 50, no. 1 (Autumn 1992).

4 Charles T. te Water to Dr. D.F. Malan, 16 December 1948, Charles Te Water Papers, A.78, Box 2, AE1/2/2. South African Archives. The authors thank Professor Lorna Lloyd for bringing this correspondance to their attention.

5 American Embassy Ottawa to Department of State, Despatch No. 45, 14 July 1952, Decimal File 601.4291/7-1452, State Department Records, United States National Archives.

6 John Hilliker, *Canada's Department of External Affairs*. Volume 1: *Coming of Age, 1909–1945* (Montreal and Kingston: McGill-Queen's University Press, 1990), 225.

7 Cited in Escott Reid, *The Radical Mandarin*, 240–1.

1 Becoming Difficult

Escott Reid's Early Years

J.L. GRANATSTEIN

Escott Reid was one of a special type of Canadian, one of the distinguished men who filled the Department of External Affairs and made it such a special place from the 1930s onward. Reid was the son of a British immigrant father and a United Empire Loyalist mother, a child of the manse imbued with the social gospel, a Rhodes Scholar who, like so many others, entrenched his Canadian nationalism at Oxford.

But Reid was atypical too. He had to drop out of high school to work as an audit clerk for the provincial government because he knew his family could not pay his way through university. That was not the case for his colleagues and friends Hume Wrong, Lester Pearson, Norman Robertson, and Arnold Heeney. Reid went to night school, saved his money, and then made his way on scholarships through Trinity College at the University of Toronto. Without the Rhodes Scholarship, he could not have gone to Oxford in 1927.

He was already a young man of the left, in full battle against conventional wisdom. This was true even in high school where he placed second in an oratorical contest with a speech on "The Future of Canada." The sixteen-year-old Reid denounced polyglot immigrants "speaking a babble of tongues, and not possessing British ideals," a conventional view in Toronto in the early 1920s, but he also called for training in English and Canadian citizenship for newcomers. He spoke of the plight of the workers and called for security against unemployment, proper housing, and the provision of "sensible means of recreation," or anything other than taverns. He fretted over the growing American influence on the Dominion's culture, called the idea of annexation "revolting to our patriotism," and pronounced an independent republic of Canada "unthinkable." What he wanted – he was sixteen years old, remember – was the abolition of appeals to the Judicial Committee of the Privy Council, an independent dominion with full control over its foreign policy, and for the schools "to build up a separate Canadian nationality with a distinctive national thought and feeling."[1]

At Trinity College, by now a fervent believer in socialism and beginning to lose his faith in God,[2] he joined that hotbed of radicalism, the Student Christian Movement, and tried to create a branch of the League for Industrial Democracy, an idea that foundered on the opposition of the university administration. He took part regularly in Hart House debates, and his socialism developed ever more strongly as his belief in his father's faith waned. He was a League of Nations man and a neutralist, and he wrote the requisite editorial in a Trinity student magazine against Remembrance Day. The dead of the First World War had died in vain, sacrificed on the altar of international anarchy, for which not just Berlin but all the Great Powers had to accept blame. The answer to preventing such anarchy in the future, Reid said, elevating the already standard clichéd arguments against war to a slightly higher plane, was not alliances and armaments but international arbitration of disputes and disarmament.[3]

Such views did not harm Reid's efforts to win a Rhodes Scholarship. He was no sportsman, but he had a strong college record with first class honours in political economy. He had also spent a summer working on a Canadian National Railways construction gang and his evenings teaching labourers to read as a Frontier College instructor. That presumably counted as much as athleticism for the selection committee, and in 1927 he was one of the two Ontario men chosen to go to Oxford.

Reid thrived at Christ Church, earning a first class honours degree in Politics, Philosophy and Economics. He enjoyed his tutors and became interested in the evolution of the Canadian party system. He joined the mainline Labour Party, but declined to sign up with the more radical Independent Labour Party, primarily because the actions of its leaders upset him more than the inaction of the Labour Party leadership. He disliked the policies of the Ramsay MacDonald government but had no qualms about defending them in a debate at the Oxford Union. He won the debate, 370 to 330, but lost the election to lead the Union. "Perhaps my tactics were bad," he lamented in a letter to a friend.[4] Even so, he was a major figure at Oxford, involved in clubs of all kinds, and he was selected to reply to the toast to the Rhodes Scholars at the annual dinner given them by the Rhodes Trust in 1930. He gave what he described as "the speech of a representative Rhodes Scholar ... composed of smugness, two parts, of brutality, one part, of tact, one part, of unctuous rectitude, one part." He lived up to his description with high good humour and ended by urging the Rhodes Trustees to increase the living allowance of Scholars – and to make this change retroactive for the three years he had been at Oxford![5]

Like most Rhodes Scholars, Reid travelled extensively. He had borrowed money to finance a two-month trip around Europe before he went up to Oxford, and he took advantage of holidays to roam. In 1928 he wrote a piece for the *Toronto Star Weekly* on "Where Mussolini Rules," and began it in superb fashion: "Castor Oil, mob law, railways running on time, suppression of the press, fewer beggars, Italianitis, noisy nationalism, a rejuvenated Italy, a menace to the Mediterranean – which of these make up the essence of fascism?"[6] It was not surprising that Reid opted correctly in the article to stress the darker side of the Mussolini regime.

His post-Oxford ambitions initially were unclear. He thought of joining the League of Nations bureaucracy in Geneva, noting sardonically that his time at Oxford had "not succeeded in killing all my enthusiasm. I am still enthusiastic about doing something for international peace."[7] But he ended by deciding to do a Ph.D. at Oxford and to work on the Canadian party system. He applied for and won a Rockefeller Foundation grant, and soon began his research at home. He decided to conduct interviews with federal and provincial politicians, bagmen, observers, and academics, and from the summer of 1930 to 1932 he travelled across Canada assembling a systematic and major oral history project, likely the first of its kind ever undertaken in Canada. A diligent man, he began his research in Winnipeg in 1930, even squeezing time out of the preparations for his wedding to interview J.W. Dafoe, the influential editor of the *Winnipeg Free Press*. There were no tape recorders, of course, but Reid wrote memoranda on each of his conversations, the best way of conducting interviews, and getting the most from them. He had no difficulty getting his subjects to spill the beans, and he seemed to have access to everyone from J.S. Woodsworth, the country's leading socialist, to T.A. Crerar, a federal cabinet minister, to Henry Wise Wood, the Alberta farm leader. His interviews are preserved in the National Archives of Canada and are not much used by historians, though they should be.[8]

Reid's dissertation, like so many then and since, was never completed,[9] but he wrote a number of excellent academic articles that together constitute a very good account – in the era before most archival collections were available – of the origins and development of Canadian political parties. Particularly notable are his paper on "The Saskatchewan Liberal Machine before 1929," and his examination of the "economic and racial bases" of the Liberal and Conservative parties.[10] These essays are still read and reprinted, and deservedly so.

The reason Reid's doctoral work ground to a halt was his appointment in 1932 as national secretary of the Toronto-based Canadian Institute of International Affairs (CIIA). Vincent Massey had made funds available for the CIIA to create a national secretary's position, and Reid, married and without a job in 1932, leapt at the chance. As it turned out, he received an offer of an appointment in the Government Department at Harvard University and would have accepted that in preference to the CIIA, but the letter of offer was sent to Winnipeg. By the time Reid received it, he had accepted the Institute position. As he said later, if he had gone to Cambridge, Massachusetts, he likely would have become involved in the New Deal and would certainly have been caught up in the McCarthy era investigations of the left.[11]

The CIIA was only four years old, a blue-ribbon group composed of former statesmen such as Sir Robert Borden and Newton Rowell, rich men like Edgar Tarr and Vincent Massey, journalists like J.W. Dafoe, and academics such as Norman MacKenzie and Henry Angus. Its aim was to encourage non-partisan interest in international affairs, and Reid's job (for which George Ferguson, managing editor of the *Winnipeg Free Press*, had suggested him to J.W. Dafoe) was to set up the Institute's national office, bring the organization to life, and make it function. In many ways, he was the right man for the job: indefatigably energetic, imaginative, well-connected, he spewed forth ideas for branches, meetings, speakers, conferences, and publications. His new job also brought him into contact with the members of the tiny Department of External Affairs. He had met the under-secretary, O.D. Skelton, in Geneva, and through Skelton he met Norman Robertson, Lester Pearson, John Read, and others. Skelton must have been impressed because, from 1933 or 1934 onward, he began to consider bringing Reid into the Department.

The CIIA, however, was no bed of roses for Reid. Its leadership was politely nationalist but fundamentally imperial-minded, capitalist, anti-socialist, and far from neutralist. Reid was a Canadian nationalist, a neutralist, and a socialist – and he made no effort to hide his views from his masters. His writings, which appeared in academic journals and in magazines such as *Canadian Forum* and *Saturday Night*, called for Canada to stay out of any future British wars and to support the League of Nations insofar as it committed Canada to nothing. He helped draft the Regina manifesto that launched the Co-operative Commonwealth Federation, and with much help from his wife Ruth – who had a strong social conscience of her own[12] – he wrote the chapter on foreign policy for the League for Social Reconstruction's book, *Social Planning for Canada*.[13] None of this pleased Borden or Massey, though it did not initially upset other, younger members such as Brooke Claxton of Montreal, a man interested in seeing a strong CIIA become a vehicle for national unity and Canadian nationalism. Nor did it concern academics such as Frank Underhill, Mackenzie, Angus, and R.A. MacKay. But many of the key players in the Institute were unhappy at the external activism and open partisanship of their secretary, though they were pleased at the way he had doubled the number of branches and tripled the Institute's membership.

Ostensibly, what upset the CIIA establishment, namely Rowell, Massey, and Dafoe, was Reid's emphasis on research and conferences. This threatened what they considered the core group of the Institute, the businessmen who had no interest in research or study groups and who, in fact, felt offended, not to say threatened, by academics and their "hi-falutin'" theories. Rowell urged his colleagues not to let Reid's "energy and enthusiasm" push the Institute away from its original purposes, and Massey, declining to offer the CIIA a grant in 1937, complained about building up the national office and "emphasizing out of its relative position those various activities which come under the heading of Research."[14]

Determined – indeed pig-headed – and suffering from his perpetual problem of an excess of zeal, Reid was unwilling to compromise, in part at least because he had the support of men such as Edgar Tarr,[15] J.M.

Macdonnell of the National Trust, and Raleigh Parkin of Sun Life Assurance, who were more than pleased by the CIIA's booming expansion under their capable national secretary and had no fear of conferences or research. In his own mind, Reid was right about the CIIA's direction and future, and that was that. Moreover, when a delegation came to see him to urge that he curtail his controversial speaking and writing on international affairs, Reid flatly refused. Even the sympathetic Claxton pronounced Reid "obdurate, obstinate and obtuse ... a fanatic and completely spoiled and undisciplined ... He called us all the emissaries of Rowell and Dafoe," Claxton wrote in 1936 after the CIIA's national council had discussed whether Reid's appointment should or could be renewed. "He refused to admit that anything he had done had injured or could injure the Institute. He said that he was serving the purpose for which he was hired ... he was free to use his spare time as he liked."[16] Reid was reappointed for a year without a raise in pay, a slap on the wrist. The next year, Dafoe himself added that Reid "is not a judicious young man."[17]

That was true enough, and it is well to remember that in 1936 Reid was just over thirty. He was a young man of extraordinary vigour, more than slightly arrogant about his intellectual powers, and completely convinced that his views were correct, certainly more so than those of the old men who ran and financed the CIIA. An agnostic in religion, Reid was a true believer in almost everything else.

In fact, the arguments over the CIIA's organization and role, while important in turning Institute opinion against Reid, were made sharper by his progressive political views, which were an anathema to the CIIA establishment. "The internationalist must be a socialist," Reid had written in his draft chapter for *Social Planning for Canada*, which was eventually published in 1935, "just as the true socialist must be an internationalist." Canada needed a socialist government – "the only hope for maintaining peace long enough for socialist governments to be established in the majority of the countries of the world."[18] In his draft of "A Foreign Policy for the C.C.F.," written in June 1934, Reid said flatly that "an unintelligent foreign policy will mean that once more will Canadian national unity be sacrificed on the altar of conscription, once more will Canadian lives be sacrificed on foreign battlefields." What was an intelligent foreign policy? Reid defined it by saying that "never again" should Canada send armed forces overseas to take part in any hostilities "whether or not the purpose of these hostilities is said to be the defence of Canada or the British Empire or the League of Nations or democracy or freedom." Moreover, he added, the League of Nations was a victors' League, and Canada should not pledge itself to apply sanctions automatically to a "so-called" aggressor.[19]

This was hard stuff to swallow for believers in collective security or the Empire. The next year, Reid went further still, calling on the government to issue a declaration "that Canada is resolved to maintain her neutrality in all future wars whoever the belligerents may be," along with a stringent neutrality act.[20] The armed forces should scrap all links with Britain, he continued, or disarm completely (they already were, in fact), and Canadian trade should be reorganized so that trans-oceanic commerce would become less important.[21] Men such as Sir Joseph Flavelle, the Toronto businessman and powerful wartime arms coordinator who propped up the CIIA's finances, were not amused, and Reid's partisan papers and speeches drove them away.[22]

When Italy threatened to attack Ethiopia in 1935, Reid continued his crusade for Canada to remain out of the pending struggle. Sovereign states were an anachronism, world government was the way of the future, and until world government was in place, the League's capacity to apply sanctions should be minimized.[23] Thus, the proper role for the League in this crisis was to create a commission to study Italy's problems and find a solution for them. If this was not done, then "sanctions under such circumstances would not be the force of equitable authority but would simply be the old-fashioned private war used by the 'haves' to assert their power against the 'have-nots.'" If Italy attacked despite the formation of a League of Nations commission, then Canada should reluctantly accept economic sanctions, but never military ones.[24] The fate of the Ethiopians presumably mattered not at all to Reid or Canada.

But League wars were far less important than a world war, and Reid was just as firmly opposed to participation here as elsewhere. In a 1937 letter to Lord Lothian, a leading British supporter of appeasement, Reid said that he believed Britain was already committed to every war waged between France and Germany, even a war in which the French were the aggressors. In his view, the Commonwealth, the Americas, and the neutral blocs of Europe should adopt a hard and fast policy of neutrality, declaring a policy of no intervention unless their territory was attacked. "I am not prepared to prescribe for any country but my own," Reid concluded, having already done just that, "but for Canada I prescribe a policy of not sending armed forces overseas under any circumstances."[25]

Neutralism was a minority opinion in Canada, outside French Canada, the Department of External Affairs, and some university departments, but Reid likely had his greatest influence on Canadian policy with his 1937 article, "Mr. Mackenzie King's Foreign Policy, 1935–1936." Pushing through the prime minister's torturous and tortured prose and deliberate bafflegab, Reid laid out the principles he saw there: the maintenance of national unity; the overriding importance to Canada not of the League but of the United States and Britain; the necessity to take a backseat on European and Asian problems; no commitment to military sanctions of the League or in defence of any part of the Commonwealth; no commitment to League economic sanctions; the necessity for Parliament to decide if Canada should participate in sanctions or war; and finally, Canadian participation in the attempt to bring international trade back to a sane basis.[26] Mackenzie King was delighted at this "excellent" article which, he wrote in his diary, "cleared my mind of many points."[27] The prime minister cited Reid's article in the House of Commons on 19 February to chide opposition members who had complained that his government had no foreign policy.[28]

The prime minister's good opinion mattered because by 1937 Reid's position at the CIIA was becoming more untenable each day, and King's goodwill as secretary of state for external affairs was critical if Reid was to be accepted into the Department of External Affairs. Reid escaped to Dalhousie University for the 1937–38 academic year, and he stepped up the desultory negotiations he had been having with Skelton about joining External Affairs. Events in Ottawa such as intense trade negotiations and fiscal concerns continued to delay an appointment, however, and it was not until December 1938 that Skelton finally won the prime minister's approval to name Reid as second secretary to the legation in Washington, at a salary of $3,900 a year plus allowances of $2,750.[29] Reid's career in External Affairs, which began the next month, would have many ups and downs, many 180-degree changes in direction, and much success.

What then are we to make of the young Escott Reid? His views in the 1930s were not uncommon in intellectual and left-wing circles, except for the force and clarity with which they were expressed. For him, as for all who had held such positions, the unmitigated evil of Hitlerism blew away the intellectual blinkers that had made neutralism seem a reasonable position during the Depression years. In his memoirs, Reid later argued that one influence on him was his belief that a balance of power existed in Europe: "I did not believe it possible that Germany could succeed in an attack on Western Europe and I agreed with the position [against Canadian participation in the war] the CCF" took in September 1939. Indeed, he wrote J.S. Woodsworth to congratulate him for his speech against war in Parliament. "When it became clear in the spring of 1940 that Germany might succeed and ... gravely endanger Canada's direct and immediate national interests, I became a supporter of all-out participation in the war," he continued in his memoirs, *Radical Mandarin*.[30] In fact, Reid remained isolationist somewhat longer than he recalled. In letters to his mother during the terrible spring of 1940, he spoke of how the Nazis had to defeat the United States before invading Canada and how no one believed that a German invasion of North America was possible. "I think we can comfort ourselves on this continent with the flattering unction that we are safe for four or five years."[31] To be fair, perhaps he was merely trying to comfort an aged parent.

If any expiation was needed, Escott Reid made up for his isolationist neutrality over the next decade by being a proponent of a strong United Nations and then, when the UN proved a weak reed, the intellectual founder of the North Atlantic Treaty. He had learned that pious preachments of unarmed neutrality were worthless in a world of predators. What he never learned, however, was to follow Norman Robertson's advice to "only pass on two-thirds of your bright ideas." In a toast to Robertson, departing for London in 1946 to become high commissioner, Reid added that "Diplomatic training has curbed my tongue and blunted my pen."[32] Regrettably for Reid, but happily for historians, it wasn't so, and Escott Reid continued to flood his superiors with memos and weary them with his moral crusades. If he had not, he wouldn't have been Escott Reid.

Escott Reid was a very intelligent man, conscious of his own gifts and conscious, too, that he was brighter than many others with whom he worked. At one point, he assessed the men he found in the Department of External Affairs when he joined at the beginning of 1939, and he preserved his notes in his personal archives. The "first rate minds," he wrote, were O.D. Skelton, Loring Christie, Hume Wrong, and Norman Robertson. The "second rate" were Lester Pearson, Arnold Heeney, then in the Prime Minister's Office, and Hugh Keenleyside.[33] Reid may well have been correct in his assessments, but he left one External Affairs officer off his list. Attached to the Prime Minister's Office, like Heeney, was Jack Pickersgill, another External Affairs officer certain of his own ability and also not averse to making judgments. To Pickersgill, Reid was an able idealist but not quite intellectually first rate. That would have upset Reid. Pickersgill added, however, that Escott Reid made his way on sheer merit, for no one loved him.[34]

Perhaps that was the fairest judgment of all, and one that Escott Reid ultimately might have agreed with. He knew he was troublesome, he knew that his fixed certainties frequently riled his colleagues and superiors and caused pain to his friends and supporters, and he understood that his almost manic energy could wear out everyone, including himself. Few loved the young (or older!) Escott Reid, but many admired the clarity of vision and enormous energy he brought to his work.

NOTES

1 Escott Reid, "The Future of Canada," 21 April 1921, vol. 4, Escott Reid Papers, National Archives of Canada (NAC). On Reid, see also my *The Ottawa Men: The Civil Service Mandarins, 1935–1957* (Toronto: Oxford University Press, 1982), chapter 8. When I examined Reid's papers there were two collections: one in the National Archives and one at Reid's home. The latter collection is referred to here as "Reid Papers (Ste Cecile de Masham, QC)." Most of these papers are now likely at the National Archives with the rest of Reid's papers.

2 Escott Reid, *Radical Mandarin: The Memoirs of Escott Reid* (Toronto: University of Toronto Press, 1989); for Reid's religious evolution, see pp. 9–10, 25, and 38.

3 Reid, *Radical Mandarin*, 33–5.

4 Escott Reid to N.A.M. MacKenzie, 15 December 1929, N.A.M. MacKenzie Papers, folder 6/4, Main Correspondence, University of British Columbia Archives (UBCA).

5 Escott Reid, "The Rhodes Scholarships," 15 June 1930, Reid Papers, vol 4, (Ste Cecile de Masham, QC).

6 21 January 1928.

7 Escott Reid to N.A.M. Mackenzie, 15 December 1929, MacKenzie Papers, folder 6/4, Main Correspondence, UBCA.

8   "Canadian Politics: Notes on Interviews, 1930–1932," Reid Papers, (Ste Cecile de Masham, QC).

9   See F.H. Underhill Papers, vol. VII, Reid file, NAC.

10 Respectively, *Canadian Journal of Economics and Political Science* II (February 1936), and *Contributions to Canadian Economics* VI (1933).

11 W.Y. Elliott to Escott Reid, 14 June 1932, Reid Papers, (Ste Cecile de Masham, QC); Reid interview, 14 October 1978. Reid also expressed this view in *Radical Mandarin*, 72.

12 Based on a conversation with Timothy Reid, 5 October 2001.

13 Research Committee of the League for Social Reconstruction, *Social Planning for Canada* (Toronto: T. Nelson, 1935).

14 Reid, *Radical Mandarin*, 78.

15 For Tarr's views on Canadian foreign policy (slightly laundered for British consumption), see "Canada in World Affairs," *International Affairs* (September, 1937), 676ff.

16 Brooke Claxton to T.W.L. MacDermot, 20 February 1936, T.W.L. MacDermot Papers, file /70, Bishop's University Archives (BUA).

17 J.W. Dafoe to Grant Dexter, 23 January 1937, Grant Dexter Papers, Queen's University Archives (QUA).

18 Michiel Horn, *The League for Social Reconstruction* (Toronto: University of Toronto Press, 1980), 146.

19 Reid Papers, vol. 4, NAC. See also Reid, "Canada and This Next War," *Canadian Forum* XIV (March 1934), 207–9; "Canada and the League," MS, 1934; and "International Sanctions and World Peace," *University of Toronto Quarterly* IV (1935), 408.

20 In February 1939 J.T. Thorson, MP, introduced a private member's bill calling for such legislation. See David Lenarcic, "Pragmatism over Principle: The Canadian Neutrality League," *Journal of Canadian Studies* XXIX (Summer 1994), 128ff.; and "Bordering on War: A Comparison of Canadian and American Neutralist Sentiment during the 1930s," *American Review of Canadian Studies* (Summer 1994), 217ff. Cf. O.M. Biggar, "Canadian Neutrality," CIIA Special Memorandum, December 1938.

21 Escott Reid, "Can Canada Remain Neutral?," *Dalhousie Review* XV (1935), 148.

22 Reid, *Radical Mandarin*, 90–2.

23 Escott Reid to Loring Christie, 10 October 1935, Reid Papers, Loring Christie file, NAC.

24 "Canada and the Ethiopian Crisis," 26 August 1935, Reid Papers, vol. 4, NAC. There is also a long memorandum by Reid and T.W.L. MacDermot, "Canada and the Ethiopian Crisis," 26 August 1935, vol. 2, Reid Papers, NAC, and two articles by Reid in *Saturday Night*: "Did Canada Cause

War?" (28 September 1935), and "League Must Give Justice as Well as Peace" (5 October 1935).

25 Escott Reid to Lord Lothian, 19 March 1939, Lothian Papers, GD40/17/349/ 545–6, Scottish Record Office.

26 *Canadian Journal of Economics and Political Science* III (February 1937), 86ff.

27 Diary, W.L.M. King Papers, 7 February 1937, file 80, NAC.

28 Reid believed King's speech had been written by Loring Christie, with whom Reid was friendly and in frequent correspondence. Reid interview, 14 October 1978. On King's foreign policy, see J.L. Granatstein and Robert Bothwell, "'A Self-Evident National Duty': Canadian Foreign Policy, 1935–1939," *Journal of Imperial and Commonwealth History* III (January 1975), 212ff.

29 Correspondence in Appointments in External Affairs Service file, Reid Papers (Ste Cecile de Masham).

30 Reid, *Radical Mandarin*, 122, 133.

31 Escott Reid to mother, 13 May and 25 June 1940, Reid Papers, vol. 20, Family Correspondence file, NAC. See David Lenarcic, "Canada's Frontier Is on the Maginot Line: Some Canadian Views on the European Balance of Power and the Fall of France," unpub. MS.

32 "Toast to Norman Robertson," 16 September 1946, Reid Papers (Ste Cecile de Masham).

33 Pen Notes, 21 July 1968, Norman Robertson file, Reid Papers (Ste Cecile de Masham).

34 J.W. Pickersgill interview, 20 February 1979.

"Writing Marginal Notes on the Pages of History"?

Escott Reid and the Founding of the United Nations, 1945–46

HECTOR MACKENZIE

From late April 1945 to mid-February 1946, Escott Reid served on Canadian delegations to the founding conference of the United Nations in San Francisco as well as to subsequent meetings of the executive committee of the preparatory commission, the preparatory commission itself, and the first session of the general assembly of the United Nations. These deliberations began while the world was still at war and ended shortly after former British prime minister Winston Churchill described the descent of an "iron curtain" dividing east from west in Europe. That a sense of futility or even despair over the onset of the Cold War should overshadow the constructive work of statesmen is less surprising than that this mood should have affected participants as early as it did. "We all have a feeling here," Reid wrote to his father in late May 1945, "that what we are doing is merely writing marginal notes on the pages of history. The substance of history is being written not in San Francisco but in Poland, Germany, Czechoslovakia, Yugoslavia and so on. That is where the new world is taking shape, and taking shape with terrifying speed."[1] For Reid and others, the breakdown of the victorious wartime alliance and the early manifestation of renewed international tensions cast a pall over negotiations that were supposed to help to build a better world – or at least a better world organization. The difficulty of determining perspective or significance affected not only the conduct and the content of the diplomacy surrounding the origins of the United Nations but also subsequent analyses.

Another challenge for anyone who examines Reid's personal involvement in this question, as with other episodes in Canada's international affairs in which he played a part, is that the main character of this story has written so much and so well himself. On this topic, Reid wrote a book – On Duty: A Canadian at the Making of the United Nations, 1945–1946[2] – and he later devoted a chapter of his memoirs, Radical Mandarin,[3] to these trials and tribulations. But that is not the end of the received version from Reid. Long before his fellow delegates had assembled in San Francisco to consider a text put forward by the great powers, the technical adviser for a middle power had written an alternative draft charter for the international organization. This remarkable document was published anonymously as a pamphlet and then extracted in the magazine Free World shortly after the conference began.[4] Although it was not endorsed by his own government and it did not have the impact for which its author had hoped, this text hovers in Reid's assessments, eclipsing the more pedestrian prose that dominated the proceedings. Moreover, Reid kept his rejected writings for later use, so that passages of his "personal charter for world sanity," as journalist James Reston labelled it, were recycled later in statements, speeches, and documents.[5] Reid also helped to write the formal reports of the Canadian delegations, which were published not long after the events that they describe.[6] Thus, we are left in little doubt about what Reid and his colleagues were doing in those months or about what Reid thought, both then and later, about their work.

Not surprisingly, Reid does not loom so large in the recollections of others. Equally unsurprising is the fact that the other Canadian participants who recorded their impressions of the formation of the United Nations, including those more senior in the delegations, were not so prolific as their diligent subordinate. In his diaries for this period Prime Minister W.L. Mackenzie King devoted considerably more attention to the national election than to the international organization, and still less to the detailed labour of the conference, from which he absented himself as soon as possible.[7] Lester B. Pearson does not mention Reid in this context in his memoirs.[8] Charles Ritchie, witty and urbane as ever, affects an air of worldly detachment in the published extracts from his diaries that deal with the formative months of the United Nations. Ritchie comments at some length in *The Siren Years* about his work in San Francisco but not at all in *Storm Signals* about the inaugural meeting of the general assembly in London.[9] Reid is not mentioned in either volume.

In other words, though he is at the centre of this paper, Reid was not the only, or even the most important, player in the dramas of which he was a part. As Lawrence Kaplan has observed, Reid was "a supporting actor whose useful hints were too frequently ignored."[10] To put it another way, Reid was a talented individual with possibly more influence on the subsequent evaluation of Canada's involvement in shaping the new international organization than on the contemporary determination of Canadian policy. Indeed, Reid often expressed his frustration at the failure of his superiors to appreciate the obvious wisdom of his preferred course of action or the vital importance of the carefully crafted phrase that he proposed to them. That is not to belittle his accomplishments nor to cast doubt on the validity of his conclusions, but rather to sound a cautionary note about what we read by Reid.

Some form of replacement for the ill-starred League of Nations – though deliberately not depicted as such – featured in statements of war aims during the Second World War, including the Atlantic Charter promulgated by Prime Minister Churchill and American President Franklin Roosevelt in August 1941. Though the United States was then still neutral, that statement pledged the wartime leaders to eight "common principles," the last of which alluded to the eventual "establishment of a wider and permanent system of general security." Curiously, the commentary on this text prepared for King by his principal adviser, the under-secretary of state for external affairs, Norman Robertson, did not even mention that vague commitment to replace the League.[11] The Atlantic Charter was subsequently endorsed by the United Nations, as the wartime allies identified themselves, in a joint declaration issued on New Year's Day, 1942.[12] Meanwhile, the concept of a global organization for collective security was elaborated further in discussions between the United Kingdom and the United States.

In March 1943 Britain's foreign minister, Anthony Eden, informed the Canadian cabinet about these recent Anglo-American talks, which sketched designs for a great-power-dominated world body.[13] During the next year King and his colleagues were keen to avoid any impression abroad or at home that Britain spoke for Canada, either in planning sessions or in the proposed authority.[14] In November 1943 the Moscow Declaration pledged the governments of the Soviet Union, the United States, and the United Kingdom to the early establishment of "a general international organization, based on the principle of the sovereign equality of all peace-loving States, and open to membership by all such States, large and small, for the maintenance of international peace and security."[15] When this subject was discussed in May 1944 by the prime ministers of the Commonwealth in London, however, the main concern of the Canadians was to pour cold water on Churchill's antiquated notion that the "British Commonwealth and Empire" would be a unified power with a single voice in any new global entity.[16]

This educational effort was repeated in Washington, where Pearson was the minister-counsellor (later ambassador) and Reid was first secretary. When the four great powers (including China) met at Dumbarton Oaks from late August to late September 1944, Pearson and Reid were among Commonwealth diplomats briefed regularly by the British representatives. They were also informed less formally and consistently by their contacts in the State Department.[17] Back in Ottawa the associate under-secretary of state for external affairs, Hume Wrong, monitored these developments as he coordinated the Canadian government's assessment under the often wary eye of his minister and prime minister, King.[18] Apart from the other consequences of this process for policy-making, such a flow of information ensured that this sometimes inharmonious trio of diplomats were cognizant of the issues and intentions long before the recommendations of the great powers were published. They were thus well-prepared to advise on a Canadian response.

The initial formal statement of Canada's position was made in a memorandum circulated in January 1945 to the four sponsoring powers and France, as well as to the dominions, Belgium, and the Netherlands. A covering note explained that the enclosure "deliberately avoids specific amendments" to the Dumbarton Oaks proposals "because there are alternative means of meeting most of the points." Even on an issue of vital interest to Canada, criteria for election to non-permanent seats on the security council, the document offered no specific solution, instead referring vaguely to the need "to devise a system of election which would provide that due regard must be paid to the international significance of the countries chosen."[19] Privately, Reid was dismayed that the Canadian government had foregone an opportunity to influence the outcome. His own preference would have been to present a revised draft charter, much as Canadian delegations had done before the meetings that founded the International Monetary Fund (IMF) and the International Civil Aviation Organization (ICAO). Indeed, Reid's personal experience with the ICAO at Chicago in late 1944 had convinced him of the advantages to be gained from that tactic.[20]

Ministers and senior officials in Ottawa, however, were not so sure and they would not endorse Reid's own attempt to second-guess the great powers. "It would be a wasted effort," Wrong opined, "for Canada as a secondary country to attempt to plan from the foundation upward."[21] With his department's permission, Reid circulated his document anonymously, but it appeared too late and was too remote from authority to influence the form of the United Nations.[22] Meanwhile, Wrong had conducted soundings in Washington and London before the delegates left for San Francisco. Those consultations reinforced his conviction that Canada's representatives must take care not to alienate the dominant powers of the wartime alliance who were sponsoring the gathering that would help to shape the post-war world.[23]

Reid was delighted to be named a technical adviser to Canada's delegation, one of a small group below the rank of ambassador. His enthusiasm was blunted when the prime minister told the Canadian participants to keep quiet and not to propose any amendments "until there was an opportunity to see how the conference developed and to ascertain what measures would be necessary."[24] For his part, Reid was convinced that the time to act was at the outset, before positions became entrenched and it was still possible to initiate change with fundamental amendments, even if compromise later proved necessary. As King and his senior advisers saw it, however, success or failure for the delegation, for the conference, and for the organization, depended on whether or not the great powers would stay in the United Nations and make it work. "Our sole preoccupation in any amendment which we may put forward or support at a later stage," King stated at the second plenary session, "will be to help in creating an organization which over the years and decades to come will be strong enough and flexible enough to stand any strains to which it may be subjected."[25] For many participants, great and small powers alike, this often meant trimming sails to take account of the strong and contrary winds emanating from the Soviet delegation. Accordingly, amendments put forward by Canada's delegation did not envisage fundamental shifts in the distribution of power or the structure of the United Nations.[26] As Pearson put it simply in a speech in early June, "Canada's preoccupation with San Francisco is based on the hard realities of the existing international situation."[27]

For Reid and other subordinates, there was more than enough work preparing for plenaries and participating in committees and sub-committees to keep them all busy. "Usually about ten of the twelve Technical Committees of the Conference meet each day," Wrong reported back to Ottawa in mid-May, "with the final batch of three sitting, as someone put it, from 8:30 p.m. until unconditional surrender." That did not even take account of the various sub-committees that had been struck. To add to the burden, Canada was represented on the three "controlling committees" – the steering committee, the executive committee, and the coordination committee – that attempted to make sense of the rest of the work. With the politicians about to depart for hustings across Canada to contest a general election, the burden of representing the country would fall on the shoulders of the officials. Thus, Reid and his colleagues found themselves with exceptional occasions for influence but without sufficient authority or latitude to take advantage of these opportunities. Before he left, King had charted a careful course for the weeks that he would be away and left Robertson in charge of Canada's delegation. "King's instructions," Reid contended, "suited Robertson's cautious temperament."[28]

Other accounts by participants and observers alike have presented a favourable image of Canada's performance at the Opera House in San Francisco, where the principal meetings took place. Certainly when contrasted to its sorry record at the League of Nations in Geneva, Canada's efforts attested to its new-found faith in constructive internationalism. With its myriad committees, the conference provided extraordinary scope for Canadian delegates to hone and to display their talents for negotiation and their skills at drafting (or redrafting). Apparently their personal contributions sufficiently enhanced the reputations of Pearson and Robertson for both to have their names later put forward by the United States for secretary-general. Even in a context in which it is difficult to assign individual or national credit for accomplishments, identifiably Canadian achievements emerged from the private meetings and plenary sessions and found their way into the Charter of the United Nations. Unfortunately, those articles most closely identified with Canada – article 23 (on criteria for election of non-permanent members of the security council), article 32 (on the participation of parties to a dispute in discussions at the security council), and article 44 (about participation in deliberations of the security council by non-members asked to contribute armed forces to a United Nations action) – have either not been invoked or they have not had their intended effects.[29]

Even so, Canada's representatives ably advanced a position that enlarged the authority of the assembly, elaborated the responsibilities of the economic and social council and enhanced the autonomy of the secretariat. In this endeavour, their efforts were focused less on drafting a perfect charter than on making the United Nations a productive and universal body, with a greater say for middle and smaller powers but without risking withdrawal by the great powers. Gordon Robertson, who was its secretary, recalls Canada's delegation as "one of the most effective at the conference," which he attributed to "the planning and preparation on policy issues" and "the exhausting effort of our senior advisers." Though it was hard work "there is no doubt that the Canadian representatives made a significant contribution to the shape of the new international organization."[30] The published Canadian report seems to back that judgment.

Yet the overall impression conveyed by Reid in his letters home and later in his published recollections is less one of accomplishments than of missed chances. He chafed at the guidance that the delegation received from the government. Reid privately complained about the prime minister's timorous leadership and the dutiful acceptance by others in the delegation (more senior to Reid) of the constraints that it imposed. In an early letter to his wife, Ruth, Reid cites King's "line" that "the Canadian delegation is to be helpful and not commit itself to rigid positions or, as Grant Dexter puts it, it is to have no principles."[31] Above all, Reid was disturbed at his government's failure to take advantage of the prestige that Canada had earned during the war and its credibility as a potential leader of the middle and smaller powers. With more envy and less irritation than some of his associates, Reid watched as the quixotic head of the Australian delegation, Herbert Evatt, tilted at the great powers.[32] From the beginning of this ordeal, when the Canadian government declined to put forward its own (or, Reid's own) comprehensive redraft of the charter, to the end, when the Soviet delegation "played their cards beautifully" to secure "the old voting formula which is so repugnant," Reid groused about disappointing results.[33]

During the conference, Reid had been drawn into detailed consideration of chapters, articles, clauses, sentences, phrases, words, and punctuation. That may have been an apt vocation for one who, according to Pearson, "would bring the Archangel Gabriel to the mat for a comma."[34] As Robertson's adviser and alternate on the coordination committee, whose task it was to reconcile the varied contributions to the charter, Reid was remarkably well placed to view the constitutional document for the organization as its elements emerged from sub-committees – often too late in the day for meaningful revision. Sometimes the muddled language and awkward phrasing were the lamentable results of a necessary compromise. Reid recalled one occasion when Robertson's quest for clarification of article 107 was met by advice from Leo Pasvolsky, the American State Department's principal expert on the Dumbarton Oaks proposals, to "let sleeping dogs lie particularly when they are such very large dogs."[35]

More often, the deficiencies of writing simply reflected the impact of collective fatigue or an inability to reach firm conclusions. Especially as delegates paid closer attention to their looming deadline, there was an understandable but unfortunate reversion to the familiar but obfuscatory phraseology of past treaties as well as a predilection to give way on disputes to dogged foes. Such a tendency aroused one of Reid's passions: a devotion to plain language with unambiguous meanings. To Reid, this was more than an academic preoccupation or pedantry, though it frequently bordered on both. Rather, it arose from a commitment to the profoundly democratic idea that treaties and other public documents – especially ones so critical to the world's future – must be understood in order to be supported. "The experience of the League of Nations in Geneva," Reid had written in introducing his own charter, "has proved that without active participation of public opinion, without understanding of what is going on in international conferences, any kind of international organization will always be threatened."[36] In his view, the best hope for humanity was popular backing for a world body that ultimately transcended or constrained the authority of national governments. For that reason, Reid was dissatisfied with the wording as well as some provisions of the charter and he was appalled at the prospect that it would be difficult to amend in the future.

Clarity, as he saw it, was especially important in the preamble. Reid's own effort had echoed the opening words of the American constitution, perhaps too closely. However, the wording of the version prepared under the direction of J.C. Smuts, the venerable prime minister of South Africa, lacked vigour. It was further marred by use of an awkward format that Reid and others identified with the ill-fated and unmourned League of Nations. Determined that the opening phrases of the new accord should rally international spirit and popular will, Reid and an Australian colleague produced a more vibrant text, which Robertson then presented to Smuts. Unfortunately, Smuts was equally devoted to his own prose and impatient to finish his work, so that the preamble remained as Smuts and his associates had written it.[37]

Reid exacted his revenge, however. The Canadian report on the San Francisco conference, the first draft of which was written by Reid, informed its readers clearly about what happened before and during the conference, with an explanatory text that followed the structure of the Charter and frankly described the Canadian positions and the fate of Canadian recommendations or amendments. The text of the Charter was examined, chapter by chapter, along with any corresponding sections of the Dumbarton Oaks proposals. Reid's commentary on the preamble was a masterpiece of oblique criticism. In effect, the second paragraph was a slight redraft of the rejected text that Reid had helped to compose. As a result, the commentary, with its emphatic statement of the purposes of the United Nations, was a considerable improvement over the preamble that it purported to describe and to justify.[38]

Much of what Reid drafted for the delegation's report may have been rejected as overly rhetorical and hortatory for a government document. Reid displayed the same fondness for "three-decker phrases," "double-barrelled ones," and "echoes from the Anglican prayer book" that annoyed Robertson during the North Atlantic Treaty negotiations two years later.[39] In some of the discarded passages, however, Reid demonstrated a realistic appraisal of the critical importance to the new organization of the participation of the great powers, so much more vital than the specific wording of the Charter, "an imperfect document." More nearly ecclesiastical in tone as well as content was the exhortation that ended "The Task Before Us":

We must be resolute and display in our just cause a holy obstinacy. We must have faith in ourselves and in each other. Above all we must remember that all men are brothers and that upon the dignity, the liberty, the inviolability of the individual men, women and children of the world depend the welfare of the people, the safety of the state, and the peace of the world.[40]

Reid was also aware that there remained much to be done.

For Reid there was little time for rest or reflection, as he set sail in early August for London. He had been named as one of the Canadian delegates to the executive committee of the preparatory commission of the United Nations, which met from 16 August to 27 October 1945. Less than a month later, the preparatory commission met, with its work not completed until shortly before Christmas. Reid remained with the delegation for the first part of the first session of the general assembly of the United Nations, though he left shortly before it concluded its work on Valentine's Day, 1946.

Canada was one of fourteen members of the executive committee, whose mandate was to draw up recommendations for the meeting of the fifty-member preparatory commission. Together, their principal tasks were to prepare procedures and agendas for the six components of the United Nations (the security council, the general assembly, the economic and social council, the trusteeship council, the international court of justice, and the secretariat) and to decide where the headquarters of the new organization should be located. Reid concentrated his efforts on three sub-committees: those dealing with the security council, the assembly, and the secretariat. In a letter to his son Patrick, written during a brief pause after the executive committee had met, Reid observed that this work "may be of more permanent value than the Charter."[41] Earlier, he had described it to his wife, Ruth, as "the most interesting job I've ever done," though it was often disheartening.[42]

Reid was convinced that the general assembly and the other organs of the United Nations must get off to a good start, with a constructive and productive first session.[43] The key to that possibility was careful preparation, including close attention to agendas, rules of procedure, and draft resolutions, all of which must emerge from the preparatory commission. The context, however, was disturbing and the pace was frustrating. With ominous developments in the world outside the committee rooms, particularly the breakdown of the wartime alliance, Reid worried "that if the proceedings of the Committee are any guide the United Nations organization will work at half the speed of the League."[44]

Near the end of the executive committee meetings, Reid commented that "one of the few cheerful things that is happening" was that "it now looks as if the Soviets are not going to blow this conference up."[45] Undoubtedly fatigue and worry about clashes between the Soviet Union and the Western powers contributed to what Reid himself described as "manic depression." Certainly his gloom was not lifted when he learned from Robertson about a Soviet spy ring operating in Canada. Though Reid claimed "that I'm not happy unless I'm working to the limit on a job I like" and his own prescription for his darkening mood was "to work harder than ever," there is little doubt that both the international situation and his exacting labours took their toll.[46] Once again, there was little time for recovery; Reid had only a brief holiday after drafting instructions for the Canadian delegation to the preparatory commission before the work of that body took up where the executive committee had left off.[47]

The formal instructions to Dana Wilgress – Canada's ambassador to the Soviet Union and the principal Canadian representative for this next phase of activity – which arrived in late November, tended to address only the specific points that had arisen in the executive committee and to leave the rest to the discretion of the delegation. The latitude of the delegates was, however, subject to the proviso that they would "of course refer for instructions any major question of policy which may arise." In one instance, a specific recommendation by Reid was explicitly rejected: "We consider that pressure for the elaboration of detailed rules of procedure and the adoption of a broad agenda for the Security Council would be largely a waste of time as the Security Council is not likely in practice to allow itself to be bound by the recommendations of the Preparatory Commission."[48] In his later writings, Reid rebutted this reasoning,[49] but at the time he had little choice but to obey. Generally speaking, the guidance was cautious and limited. Needless to say, Reid disagreed with this approach. Though his authority and status were greater in this gathering and he worked well with Wilgress, Reid believed that much more could have been accomplished with greater freedom of action.

In his report to Ottawa when the meetings were over, Wilgress agreed with Reid's observation "that if Canada sends to a general international conference a competent and hard-working delegation, it becomes almost automatically one of the Big Five of the conference." In London, the combination of parliamentarians and civil servants had been formidable. In most instances, the conclusions reached by the preparatory commission on controversial issues were compromises, often engineered discreetly by the British and American representatives so as to avoid destructive clashes with the Soviet delegates. The most significant achievement of the preparatory commission had been to lay the groundwork for an efficient beginning to the work of the United Nations. This had been made possible by its decision not simply to "rubber-stamp at plenary sessions the Executive Committee's Report" but instead to advance its own work in sub-committees, an arrangement attributed to Reid's influence. Perhaps that personal contribution, as well as the practical advances made in less than a month, help to explain an apparent improvement in Reid's mood at this time.[50]

As the task of the preparatory commission neared its end, Reid pronounced himself "tired but happy." What had kept him so busy in San Francisco and London, he wrote to Ruth, "has been really creative and encouraging. If we can only keep on building the international order at the rate of the last five months we may be able to depart in peace from this world." In contrast to his earlier remarks about the slow pace and about the frustrations of drafting and redrafting, Reid seemed more pleased with his own role and with the outcome.

I think I'm more sure of myself, more at peace with myself because I've been able to create – even if the final product is anonymous. I am more hopeful of the future because one experiment in the possibility of two worlds working together has succeeded even though most of the other experiments taking place at the same time have failed. So far as the United Nations is concerned we have only reached the end of the beginning but at least we have got there without mishap.[51]

Reid even saw a silver lining in the dark clouds of delay prompted by lengthy debates, as these discussions may have furthered mutual understanding, if not agreement, notably about differing approaches to "international administration." Reid was especially keen that the delegation to the inaugural meeting of the general assembly should be told to resist any interpretation of the Charter that would restrict the powers of the assembly. That meant also "pressing for the election of competent chairmen in the main committees" rather than going along with any slate put forward by the great powers. Perhaps Canada and "other responsible middle powers" could collaborate to promote "contested elections in all the main committees."

How Canada itself would fare in elections to the economic and social council and to the security council – both of which would take place in the general assembly – was still uncertain after all this time. Thus, "the calibre of the Canadian Delegation to the Assembly" was especially important. "Canada's chances of election," Reid advised, "will also of course be affected by the general position it takes in the Assembly in controversies between the Great Powers and the smaller powers. If Canada swings too much to the support of the Great Power positions it may lose more small power votes than it will gain from the votes of Great Power satellites." In the meetings in London, "Canada has steered a middle course, and has been against the Great Powers about as frequently as it has voted with them. It is to be hoped that this situation will continue." When he published extracts from this report nearly forty years later, Reid editorialized parenthetically that "It didn't."[52]

When he learned who would represent Canada in the general assembly, Reid was disappointed. He had hoped that the delegation would be led by King, St Laurent, and Brooke Claxton, an associate from Reid's earlier days with the Canadian Institute of International Affairs who was now minister of national health and welfare. Instead, he was informed that the members of the cabinet who would be spared for this duty were St Laurent, the minister of agriculture, Jimmy Gardiner, and the secretary of state, Paul Martin. The other delegates were senior diplomats with whom Reid had clashed in the past: Vincent Massey, Canada's high commissioner in London, and Wrong.[53] In early December Reid was nominated by Robertson as one of ten advisers to the delegation with the observation that "he is more competent than any other Canadian on the whole range of problems of organization."[54] Reid was also the only one who had participated throughout the deliberations. Wilgress, who had so ably (and from Reid's point of view congenially) led Canada's team at the preparatory commission, shared Reid's disappointment that King would not attend the opening of the general assembly. "His presence might help our chances of election to both Security Council and Economic and Social Council," Wilgress advised Robertson. "While we are reasonably certain of election to Security Council on account of our participation in development of Atomic energy, we cannot count with assurance on election to Economic and Social Council."[55]

By year's end and before the assembly met, the cumulative effects of tiring and stressful work had finally overtaken Reid, who checked himself into a Canadian military hospital to recover from what he correctly diagnosed as exhaustion. On his return to work, he read for the first time the instructions for the delegation that had been prepared in Ottawa under Wrong's direction.[56] Reid had hoped that when the general assembly met the Canadians would steer an independent course, opposing poor candidates proposed by the great powers as chairmen of committees, pushing for secret ballots in elections to thwart Soviet efforts to manipulate the process, and voting "for the best possible candidates for the Economic and Social Council, regardless of the big power slates."[57] Wrong preferred a cautious approach that would not imperil Canada's coveted election to the security council. This view was reflected not only in the formal guidance but also in his advice and conduct after he arrived in London. In spite of the care thus taken – or possibly, as Reid believed, because of it – Canada narrowly failed to gain that laurel when balloting took place. Instead, incautious Australia, which had made such an impression in San Francisco and which also had a geographic advantage over Canada, was elected to the security council. Canada had to be consoled with an overwhelming election to a three-year term on the economic and social council and a membership on the atomic energy commission.[58] Wrong's rejection of Reid's counsel was consistent with a pattern that held over the next month.

For Reid, it was a frustrating experience to have his recommendations ignored or discounted. After so many months of hard work and with so much expertise developed in the unglamorous setting of the committees, he was particularly upset when the task of preparing St Laurent's speech for the opening debate in the general assembly was assigned to Ritchie, who evidently did not make use of Reid's draft remarks and whose text was inoffensive and uninspiring. Clearly the bloom was off the rose when Reid wrote to Ruth near the end of January. Reid was bored by working in committees that "are merely rubber-stamping" the report of the preparatory commission. "I did more in a week in the Executive Committee to influence the future of the United Nations," he claimed, "than the whole Canadian delegation will do in the four weeks of the Assembly." Already Reid had resolved to ask Robertson not to assign him to the same conferences as Wrong, who "makes a deliberate point of neither asking nor taking my advice." Cast in a bit part, Reid left before the session adjourned.[59]

Though this was evidently a disappointing conclusion to his involvement in the establishment of the United Nations, Reid still believed that the effort had been worthwhile and that the result, with all its uncertainties and flaws, made the world a better and a safer place. Wrong was not so sure. In his view, Soviet use of the initial gatherings of the new forum to score propaganda points had not only severely strained "the effective operation of the Charter at its first trial" but had also made "it apparent that talk of turning the United Nations into an agency of international government, by the delegation to it of a portion of the sovereignty of the members, is in present conditions wholly unrealistic." But what most provoked Reid's ire was his superior's glib observation in a draft of his retrospective commentary that "the first meetings of the Security Council and the Assembly leave open the question whether the establishment of the United Nations has in fact furthered its primary purpose – the maintenance of international peace and security." Reid's rejoinder is worth quoting, not only for its content but also as a manifestation of Reid's unquenchable spirit and relentless argumentation:

In order to say that the question is open you must be able to argue that the present situation would be no worse if the United Nations had not been established. Is it possible to maintain this? Presumably the "attitude towards each other of the great powers" would have been about the same if the United Nations had not existed. They would either have continued to meet at five or three-power meetings and quarrelled (with the quarrels getting out in the press) or they would not have met and would have quarrelled through diplomatic channels and by open Soviet abuse in their press and radio countered by public statements by the leaders of the Western powers. So far as I can judge the quarrels would have gone on anyway, and the existence of the United Nations has not made them worse. On the other hand the existence of the United Nations has already done some good and may do much more good in matters not directly related to their quarrels.

This may have been typical of Reid; Wrong's response was equally in character. Rather than change his mind or rephrase a word of his text, Wrong simply observed in his covering note that "Reid takes a more cheerful view than I do of the proceedings in the Security Council."[60]

Looking back from the summer of 1947, Reid commented that "most of us had hoped before San Francisco that the Charter would be less imperfect than it is." Still, as he observed, the document "represents the greatest possible measure of agreement which could then be reached between the great powers and that probably they were able to reach a greater measure of agreement then than they could today."[61] In that process, Canada made a difference, though not as great a one as Reid would have wanted. The cautious and conciliatory – even deferential – approach taken by Canada may have cost some plaudits and perhaps votes for the security council, but it arguably did no harm to the United Nations nor to Canada's principal allies in the developing Cold War. A more bold and forthright policy and a better Charter might have been more satisfying for Reid and for later commentators, but it is questionable whether the United Nations would have functioned better, or if its improved performance would necessarily have altered the drift in world affairs toward bipolar confrontation. In that sense, Reid's observation about "writing marginal notes on the pages of history" may well be appropriate.

But that does not diminish the fact that this was a worthwhile endeavour and that Reid played his assigned part well. John Holmes described him as "a major and dynamic force" in London "during the summer and autumn of 1945 when the Preparatory Commission and the Executive Committee were meeting in Westminster." According to Holmes, "Reid was a superb and compulsive draftsman, with a zealous sense of mission about international organization."[62] At the end of this wearying process, Reid may have felt ignored or underappreciated, particularly by Wrong, but it is worth noting that his relentless and righteous pursuit of his aims did not harm his career at this time. On the contrary, Reid rose rapidly to the senior ranks of the Department of External Affairs; within three years of the meetings in London he was its acting deputy minister.[63]

As others have attested and as Reid himself conceded, he was not always an easy colleague. He was ever ready to resume a struggle for what he perceived to be a just cause – continuing several conflicts in his memoirs. Jack Granatstein has observed that Reid approached his numerous crusades "with equal zeal and a missionary fervour that exhausted those around him."[64] But he was valued by Pearson for those qualities that had prompted O.D. Skelton to recruit him to the foreign service in the first place.[65] As Geoffrey Pearson has written in a volume about his father's diplomacy, Reid was "at once gadfly, philosopher, and 'holy obstinat,'" whose contribution was vital to Mike Pearson and to the Department of External Affairs.[66] The department – and arguably the United Nations as well – were better places as a result of his presence, his his commitment, his abiding humanity, and his determination to improve the prospects for future generations.

NOTES

1   Escott Reid to A.J. Reid, 24 May 1945, in Escott Reid, *On Duty: A Canadian at the Making of the United Nations, 1945–1946* (Toronto: University of Toronto Press, 1983), 49–50; Charles Ritchie, *The Siren Years: A Canadian Diplomat Abroad, 1937–1945* (Toronto: Macmillan, 1974), 202 (diary, 28 June 1945).

2   Reid, *On Duty*, 49–50.

3   Escott Reid, *Radical Mandarin* (Toronto: University of Toronto Press, 1989), chapter 14.

4   [Escott Reid], "Free World Recommends A Charter for the United Nations," *Free World* [May 1945], 77–83.

5   James Reston, writing in the *New York Times*, 28 March 1969, cited in both Reid, *On Duty*, 18, and in Reid, *Radical Mandarin*, 191.

6   Department of External Affairs (DEA), *Conference Series, 1945, No. 2, Report on the United Nations Conference on International Organization Held at San Francisco, 25th April – 26th June, 1945* (Ottawa: King's Printer, 1945); DEA, *Conference Series, 1946, No. 1, Report on the First Part of the First Session of the General Assembly of the United Nations Held in London, January 10 – February 14, 1946* (Ottawa: King's Printer, 1946). These reports are referred hereinafter respectively as: DEA, *San Francisco Report*; DEA, *London Report*. One of the first scholarly reflections by a participant on Canada's part in the formation of the United Nations was Reid's address delivered to a conference of the Canadian Institute on Public Affairs in August 1947 that was later published as "Canada's Role in the United Nations." This speech, with its regretful tone about the evident failings of the new international organization and particularly about the debilitating effect of the use of the veto by the great powers, is often also cited as a precursor to the "Canadian crusade" for the North Atlantic Treaty. Escott Reid, "Canada's Role in the United Nations," in Eugene A. Forsey, ed., *Canada in a New World* (Toronto: Ryerson Press, 1948), 29–42; Hector Mackenzie, "Canada, the Cold War and the Negotiation of the North Atlantic Treaty," in John Hilliker and Mary Halloran, eds, *Diplomatic Documents and Their*

Users (Ottawa: Department of Foreign Affairs and International Trade, 1995), 145–73.

7   There are lengthy extracts from King's diaries (which are now part of the W.L.M. King Papers at the National Archives of Canada) in J.W. Pickersgill and D.F. Forster, eds, *The Mackenzie King Record, Volume 2, 1944–1945* (Toronto: University of Toronto Press, 1968), 375–434.

8   Lester B. Pearson, *Mike: The Memoirs of the Right Honourable Lester B. Pearson, Volume I, 1897–1948* (Toronto: University of Toronto, 1972), 264–78.

9   Ritchie, *Siren Years*, 187–204; Charles Ritchie, *Diplomatic Passport: More Undiplomatic Diaries, 1946–1962* (Toronto, Macmillan, 1981).

10 In foreword to *On Duty*, ix.

11 David R. Murray, ed., *Documents on Canadian External Relations* [hereafter *DCER*], *Volume 7: 1939–1941 Part I* (Ottawa: Information Canada, 1974), 237–9: Dominions Secretary to High Commissioner of Great Britain, Circular Telegram z.259, 13 August 1941; Memorandum from Under-Secretary of State for External Affairs (USSEA) to Prime Minister (PM), 14 August 1941.

12 John F. Hilliker, ed., *DCER, Volume 9: 1942–43* (Ottawa: Information Canada, 1980), 99–102: Draft declaration, n.d.; Memorandum from USSEA to PM, 29 December 1941; Memorandum from USSEA to PM, 31 December 1941. See also Government of Canada, *Treaty Series*, 1942, No. 1.

13 Pearson, *Mike*, 1: 265–6.

14 J.L. Granatstein, *A Man of Influence: Norman A. Robertson and Canadian Statecraft, 1929–68* (Toronto: Deneau, 1981), 143–7.

15 Quoted in DEA, *San Francisco Report*, 7; Pearson, *Mike*, 1: 266–7.

16 John Hilliker, ed., *DCER, Volume 11: 1944–1945, Part II* (Ottawa: Supply and Services Canada, 1990), 606–15: Statement by PM, 11 May 1944; Memorandum by First Secretary, High Commission in Great Britain, [*ca* 17 May 1944]. James Eayrs, *In Defence of Canada: Peacemaking and Deterrence* (Toronto: University of Toronto Press, 1972), 140–2.

17 Pearson, *Mike*, 1: 268–71.

18 John Hilliker, *Canada's Department of External Affairs, Volume 1, The Early Years, 1909–1946* (Montreal and Kingston: McGill-Queen's University Press, 1990), 305.

19 Hilliker, *DCER* 11: 680–5: Secretary of State for External Affairs (SSEA) to High Commissioner in Great Britain (HCGB), Telegram 89, 12 January 1945; SSEA to HCGB, Telegram 90, 12 January 1945; Ambassador in United States to SSEA, Despatch 100, 15 January 1945.

20 David MacKenzie, *Canada and International Civil Aviation 1932–1948* (Toronto: University of Toronto Press, 1989), 146–51; A.F.W. Plumptre, *Three*

Decades of Decision: Canada and the World Monetary System, 1944–75 (Toronto: McClelland and Stewart, 1977), 36–42; Reid, *Radical Mandarin*, 191–3.

21 Hilliker, *DCER* 11: 1–3: Memorandum by Assistant USSEA, 23 February 1944. Eayrs, *Peacemaking and Deterrence*, 144. Tom Keating, *Canada and World Order: The Multilateralist Tradition in Canadian Foreign Policy* (Toronto: McClelland and Stewart, 1993), 26–7.

22 Reid, *On Duty*, 18–23.

23 Hilliker, *DCER* 11: 692–6, 732–7, 740–7: Memorandum from Associate USSEA to PM, 15 February 1945; [Canadian Delegation], "Questions Arising from the Dumbarton Oaks proposals Put Forward for Discussion by the Canadian Delegation," 5 April 1945; HCGB to SSEA, Telegram 1020, 10 April 1945 (from Wrong); HCGB to SSEA, Telegram 1053, 13 April 1945 (from Wrong); HCGB to SSEA, 23 April 1945 (Massey to Robertson).

24 Hilliker, *DCER* 11: 751: Minutes of Meeting of Canadian Delegation, United Nations Conference on International Organization, 27 April 1945.

25 DEA, *San Francisco Report*, 10–12.

26 Hilliker, *DCER* 11: 755-60: "Amendments to Dumbarton Oaks Proposals Suggested by the Canadian Delegation," 4 May 1945.

27 Lester B. Pearson, *Words and Occasions* (Toronto: University of Toronto, 1970), 62–6.

28 Hilliker, *DCER* 11: 765–79: H.H. Wrong to John Read, 13 May 1945; Secretary, Delegation to United Nations Conference [R.G. Robertson], Memorandum, 14 May 1945 (with several enclosures). Reid, *Radical Mandarin*, 195.

29 Hector Mackenzie, "Myth and Reality of Canada's 'Internationalism' – from the League of Nations to the United Nations," Public Lecture, Carleton University, 3 November 2001; Granatstein, *Man of Influence*, 155; J.W. Pickersgill and D.F. Forster, eds, *The Mackenzie King Record, Volume 3: 1945–46* (Toronto: University of Toronto Press, 1970), 62; C.P. Stacey, *Canada and the Age of Conflict: A History of Canadian External Policies, Volume 2: 1921–1948, The Mackenzie King Era* (Toronto: University of Toronto Press, 1981), 384–5; Reid, *Radical Mandarin*, 199–200.

30 Gordon Robertson, *Memoirs of a Very Civil Servant: Mackenzie King to Pierre Trudeau* (Toronto: University of Toronto Press, 2000), 45.

31 Escott Reid to Ruth Reid, 25 April 1945, quoted in Reid, *On Duty*, 28–9.

32 There is an excellent account of Evatt's role in Paul Hasluck, *Diplomatic Witness: Australian Foreign Affairs 1941–1947* (Melbourne: Melbourne University Press, 1980), chapter 19. See also Herbert Vere Evatt, *The United Nations* (Cambridge, Mass.: Harvard University Press, 1948).

33 Escott Reid to Ruth Reid, 8 June 1945, quoted in Reid, *On Duty*, 59.

34 John Holmes, *The Shaping of Peace: Canada and the Search for World Order, 1943–1957, Volume 1* (Toronto: University of Toronto Press, 1979), 262.

35 Reid, *On Duty*, 47.

36 [Reid], "Free World Recommends," 77–83. Reid, "Canada's Role," 37; Ritchie, *Siren Years*, 200–1 (diary entry for 18 June 1945).

37 Escott Reid to Ruth Reid, 19 June 1945, quoted in Reid, *On Duty*, 62–3. See the discussion of the text in Reid, *Radical Mandarin*, 198–9. Hasluck, *Diplomatic Witness*, 199–200.

38 DEA, *San Francisco Report*, 16; Reid, *Radical Mandarin*, 199.

39 Hector Mackenzie, ed., *DCER, Volume 14: 1948* (Ottawa: Canada Communication Group, 1994), 640–1: High Commissioner in United Kingdom to SSEA, Telegram 1987, 9 November 1948 (Robertson to Reid).

40 Reid, *On Duty*, 66–8.

41 Escott Reid to Patrick Reid, quoted in Reid, *On Duty*, 75.

42 Escott Reid to Ruth Reid, 20 September 1945, quoted in Reid, *On Duty*, 90.

43 Hilliker, *DCER 11*: 802–4: Alternate Representative, Executive Committee, United Nations Preparatory Commission [Escott Reid], to SSEA, No. 7, 24 August 1945.

44 Escott Reid to Ruth Reid, 12 October 1945, quoted in Reid, *On Duty*, 93.

45 Escott Reid to Ruth Reid, 24 October 1945, quoted in Reid, *On Duty*, 96.

46 Escott Reid to Ruth Reid, 20 September 1945; Escott Reid to Ruth Reid, 31 October 1945, quoted in Reid, *On Duty*, 90, 97.

47 "Draft Memorandum on the Nature of the Instructions which might be given to the Canadian Delegation to the Preparatory Commission," 2 November 1945, extracted in Reid, *On Duty*, 101–3. Hilliker, *DCER 11*: 851–63: [Draft] "Report by the Canadian Delegation on the Work of Executive Committee of the Preparatory Commission of the United Nations Held at London, 16th August–22nd November, 1945," 22 November 1945.

48 Hilliker, *DCER 11*: 872–4: SSEA to HCGB, Telegram 2791, 27 November 1945 (for Wilgress).

49 Reid, *On Duty*, 146–8.

50 Hilliker, *DCER 11*: 895–902: Representative, United Nations Preparatory Commission [L.D. Wilgress] to USSEA, 14 January 1946, enclosing "Report by Representative, United Nations Preparatory Commission," 4 January 1946.

51 Escott Reid to Ruth Reid, 22 and 24 December 1945, quoted in Reid, *On Duty*, 122.

52 "Comments on Work of Preparatory Commission," 28 December 1944, reprinted in Reid, *On Duty*, 126–30.

53 Escott Reid to Ruth Reid, 31 December 1945, quoted in Reid, *On Duty*, 131; J.L. Granatstein, *The Ottawa Men: The Civil Service Mandarins, 1935–1957* (Toronto: Oxford University Press, 1982), 239–47.

54 Donald M. Page, ed., *DCER, Volume 12: 1946* (Ottawa: Supply and Services Canada, 1977), 656–8: Memorandum from USSEA to PM, 5 December 1945.

55 Page, *DCER* 12: 658–9: HCGB to SSEA, Telegram 3747, 24 December 1945, Secret and Personal (Wilgress to Robertson).

56 Page, *DCER* 12: 659–70: Memorandum by Associate USSEA, 7 January 1946, enclosing "Instructions for the Delegation to the General Assembly of the United Nations," 27 December 1945.

57 Escott Reid to Ruth Reid, 13 January 1946, quoted in Reid, *On Duty*, 136.

58 F.H. Soward, *Canada in World Affairs, From Normandy to Paris, 1944–1946* (Toronto: Oxford University Press, 1950), 152–4; Hasluck, *Diplomatic Witness*, 246–51; Reid, *On Duty*, 134–5; James Eayrs, *In Defence of Canada*, 166–7; Holmes, *Shaping of Peace*, vol. 1: 265–8.

59 Escott Reid to Ruth Reid, 18 January 1946 and 28 January 1946, quoted in Reid, *On Duty*, 137–40. DEA, *London Report*, Appendix A (pp. 57–61).

60 Page, *DCER* 12: 673–80: Hume Wrong to Norman Robertson, 2 March 1946; Hume Wrong, "Impressions of the First General Assembly of the United Nations," 27 February 1946. Escott Reid to Hume Wrong, 25 February 1946, reprinted in Reid, *On Duty*, 159–61.

61 Reid, "Canada's Role," 30–1.

62 Holmes, *Shaping of Peace*, 1: 262.

63 Granatstein, *Man of Influence*, 206.

64 Ibid.

65 John Hilliker, *Canada's Department of External Affairs, Volume 1, The Early Years, 1909–1946*, 191. Skelton's recruitment of Reid is discussed in J.L. Granatstein, "Becoming Difficult: Escott Reid's Early Years," in this volume.

66 Geoffrey A.H. Pearson, *Seize the Day: Lester B. Pearson and Crisis Diplomacy* (Ottawa, 1993), 9–10; Geoffrey Pearson, "Escott Reid: Diplomat and Scholar," *Behind The Headlines* 57, no. 1.

3

Escott Reid, the North Atlantic Treaty, and Canadian Strategic Culture

DAVID G. HAGLUND AND STÉPHANE ROUSSEL

Borrowing from Kant and Bismarck

In the historiography of Canadian foreign policy, Escott Reid is chiefly associated with the creation of the North Atlantic Alliance, and in particular with article 2 of the Washington Treaty, the "Canadian article" that urged alliance members to collaborate on the social and economic challenges confronting them. Not only was he one of the first to raise the possibility of forming such an alliance (during a conference held at Lake Couchiching on 13 August 1947), but he also participated, from Ottawa, in every phase of the negotiations. The history of these discussions and the nature of Reid's contribution are well known, at least among Canadian commentators, Reid himself having left many accounts of these events.[1]

Reid left behind an enduring achievement in the form of the Atlantic Alliance itself, but his conception of transatlantic relations and the place that Canada occupied in them has also done much to shape the way that Canadians *think* and *talk* about the North Atlantic Treaty Organization (NATO). In particular, during the 1940s, Reid developed and refined the idea that the Atlantic Alliance would provide Ottawa with a "counterweight" to the growing influence of the United States. Since then, this concept has become part of the common vocabulary of Canadian foreign policy.

Indeed, Reid's notion of a counterweight is part of a set of dominant ideas, images, and metaphors[2] that have persisted over time and helped guide the decisions of Canadian leaders (even after the original conditions that led to their development have disappeared), which is sometimes referred to as a "strategic culture." This culture is a conditioning category (Colin Gray refers to it as a "context")[3] that enables us to comprehend better the basis of decision-making relating to the use (or non-use, as the case may be) of military force in pursuit of the attainment of state objectives. It is, in the words of Alastair Iain Johnston, an "ideational milieu" that conditions state behaviour in ways nevertheless congruent with notions of "rationality." It consists, he explains, in an integrated "system of symbols (e.g., argumentative structures, languages, analogies, metaphors) which acts to establish pervasive and long-lasting strategic preferences by formulating concepts of the role and efficacy of military force in interstate political affairs, and by clothing these conceptions with such an aura of factuality that the strategic preferences seem uniquely realistic and efficacious."[4]

Strategic culture is a subset of the broader, umbrella category of "political culture," a somewhat hazy entity that occupies uncertain (if vital) terrain between psychological and structural accounts of political causality. What makes political culture "cultural" is its symbolic content, with symbols being the cognitive devices developed by human collectivities to "transmit meanings from person to person despite vast distances of space and time."[5] Central to this understanding of political culture is what the poet T.S. Eliot once referred to as "objective correlatives" – that is, vehicles such as imagery and metaphor so essential for establishing meaning, because they serve as the "depository of widespread interest and feeling," to use Lowell Dittmer's words.[6]

Much has been written about the transatlantic "counterweight," and it is for precisely this reason that this metaphor can be regarded as a component of Canada's strategic culture. The first objective of this chapter is to demonstrate how Reid contributed to entrenching this metaphor in Canadian discourse about the Atlantic Alliance and how this metaphor was subsequently sustained in that discourse. This persistence is surprising in itself because, as we shall see, the policies inspired by this metaphor have only rarely achieved their objectives.

This chapter also tries to resolve what appears to be, in theoretical terms, a contradiction in Reid's thinking. On one hand, the formulation of the counterweight metaphor reflects a "realist" conception of international relations, based essentially on the primacy of power relations and national interest, on the conflictual dimension of relations between states, and on the anarchic character of the international system. From this perspective, the counterweight to American influence would arise from the existence of a kind of *balance of power*. Yet on the other hand, Reid's ideas also seem tinged with idealism. For example, the proposal for a "North Atlantic community" that underlies the wording of article 2 is based on establishing global standards for achieving social justice, on regulating international relations through institutions, and on promoting trade. In short, Reid seems to borrow as much from Bismarck as from Kant![7]

How then should we position Reid on the intellectual map? To attempt to do so by drawing a strict distinction between "idealism" and "realism" would probably be a mistake. In fact, Reid would appear to be a representative of a now forgotten intellectual current known as "liberal realism," and by viewing his thought and actions through this lens we can resolve this contradiction. The last part of this paper is therefore devoted to a brief review of this approach, thus enabling us to present Reid not only as a "producer" of strategic culture, but also as a product of his time.

The Problem and the Solution

In March 1941, while posted to the Canadian Legation in Washington, Reid wrote to the legal advisor of the Department of External Affairs, Loring Christie:

The way things are going at present it seems probable that after the war the people of [the U.S.] will be fairly well agreed that they have a "national mission" to organize this hemisphere politically and economically ... My guess is that Canada's best chance of maintaining a fair degree of real autonomy after the war is to push as hard as possible for a federalization of matters which are of joint concern to Canada and the United States ... The more joint organs for the administration of common interests, the better are our chances of having some influence over the United States policies which affect us.[8]

In his memoirs Reid comments on this letter in these terms: "For the rest of my life, I would search for ways by which we might influence United States' policies which affect us."[9] In fact, this letter describes not only the nature of the problem that was to obsess him for the rest of his life, but also the foundations of the solution that he would attempt to promote to solve it.

Where did Reid's fear of the United States come from, and when did it first emerge? It seems that Reid's conception of international relations – and more specifically, Canada–US relations – began to evolve in the mid-1930s. As historian J.L. Granatstein observes, the adolescent Reid was attracted by plans for world disarmament and the use of arbitration to settle conflicts. Subsequently he adopted a neutralist stance on Canadian foreign policy, influenced by the social democratic ideas of Frank Underhill and Frank Scott, which led him to characterize the League of Nations as a "league of the capitalist powers."[10] Reid was not terribly worried that another war in Europe might erupt and again force young Canadians to fight overseas. Rather, he was confident that an effective balance of power – not some international institution – would guarantee peace![11]

Reid's ideas naturally led him to distrust the United States, not only because it was one of these capitalist powers, but also because he foresaw the likely consequences for North American relations of the neutralist policy that he was promoting. However, it was only after his posting to the Canadian Legation in Washington in 1941 that Reid's concerns about the power and influence of the United States finally became central to his strategic thinking. Of course Reid was never alone in expressing fears about United States influence during the 1930s and the first few years of the Second World War. The federal Conservative Party, for instance, wedded to all things British, traditionally articulated such worries.[12] However, after the Japanese attack on Pearl Harbor on 7 December 1941, the debate over relations with the US grew much sharper in official Ottawa. As early as the end of December 1941, Norman Robertson, Canada's under-secretary of state for external affairs, and Hugh Keenleyside, assistant under-secretary, noted a harsh stiffening in Washington's attitude toward Canada and worried about an appropriate Canadian response.[13]

Their views obviously struck a sensitive chord with Reid, who produced his own memorandum in January 1942 with the evocative title "The United States and Canada: Domination, Cooperation, Absorption."[14] According to Denis Smith, "Reid carried the discussion beyond the fatalism of Robertson and Keenleyside, focusing on Canadian responsibility for her own plight and offering a vision of how Canada might escape from the status of a helpless dependent power."[15] One of the proposals that Reid made in this memorandum echoed his letter of March 1941. "The present trend towards the domination of Canada's external policy by the United States is the sort of thing to be expected under present conditions. Under a collective system a small state like Canada would have an opportunity to exert a reasonable amount of influence in international politics at the cost of putting various aspects of its sovereignty into an international pool."[16]

Reid reiterated these views throughout the war, particularly in memoranda dispatched in April 1943 and February 1944.[17] In the first of these, he expressed the belief that Canada would have no choice but to continue its military co-operation with the United States after the war, especially in a context where a confrontation with the Soviet Union was becoming more and more likely:

It would be easier and more self-respecting for Canada to give up to an international body on which it was represented the decision on when it should go to war than to transfer the right to make that decision from the government in Ottawa to the government in Washington ... It would thus appear probable that effective military cooperation between Canada and the United States is possible only within the framework of an effective world order of which both Canada and the United States are loyal members.[18]

During the war, Reid seems to have been the only one to have raised the idea, at least in such a systematic fashion, that the troubling influence of the United States in Canadian security affairs should be diluted through a far broader arrangement. Yet this idea was not completely new. In fact, it found fertile ground in another metaphor that had emerged in the mid-1920s and was gaining popularity in the 1940s: the "North Atlantic triangle."[19] Until the Second World War, this metaphor was used mainly to express Ottawa's ability to play London off against Washington – and vice-versa – in the diplomatic and economic spheres. The idea of seeking a counterweight was thus implicit in the use of this concept.[20]

Counterweights and balances of power are among the oldest concepts in international relations, and can be traced to the eighteenth-century writings of such authors as Emmerich von Vattel and David Hume. What was original about Reid's proposals was the way in which he adapted the concepts of the North Atlantic triangle and the counterweight to the realities of the moment, an adaptation that illustrates the liberal/realist duality in his thinking. On one hand, Reid substituted Western Europe for Great Britain as the third element in the North Atlantic triangle. On the other, and this was his most important contribution, he situated the counterweight far more in international institutions than in individual states. This institutionalist commitment, clearly apparent in Reid's writings throughout the war, reflected the idealist – if not Utopian – dimension of his concept of international relations.

The Transatlantic Balance of Power

The conclusion of the Second World War did not mark the end of Ottawa's concern over relations with the United States. Indeed, as the Cold War intensified in 1945 and 1946, Ottawa's worries grew. In the event of a con-frontation with the USSR, Canadian territory would assume vital strategic importance, and many feared that Washington would show little regard for Canadian sovereignty if the security of American soil was at stake.[21] These developments led the Canadian government to seek an institutional framework in which it could more effectively manage relations with its well-meaning but sometimes troublesome neighbour. Initially Reid and his colleagues hoped to find this framework in the new United Nations. Reid participated directly in the negotiations leading to the creation and establishment of the UN, but this episode seems to have undermined his commitment to world institutions. The special status that the five great powers reserved for themselves and the obstreperous behaviour of the Soviet delegation stripped away his illusions. "The UN man, the believer in the Utopian world of international organization in which Canada could find safety and prosperity," remarks Granatstein, "had begun to be replaced by the anti-Soviet hard-liner."[22]

In the spring of 1946, when he returned to Ottawa to head the European branch at External Affairs, Reid readjusted his sights. He was not, despite his deep disappointment, overcome by the failure of the UN to provide a balance to the United States. Instead, he adapted his ideas and developed a new framework for putting them into practice. Drawing on a memorandum that he had written in February 1947, as well as on a report by the Joint Intelligence Committee, a memorandum by Dana Wilgress, and George Kennan's famous article on the nature of Soviet diplomacy,[23] Reid prepared the document that probably best sums up his vision of international relations and that led him to become one of the main promoters of the Atlantic Alliance. "The United States and the Soviet Union: A Study of the Possibility of War and Some of the Implications for Canadian Policy"[24] was distributed at the end of August 1947, two weeks after Reid had, in a speech at Lake Couchiching, unveiled publicly for the first time his idea for an alliance of western states to combat Soviet aggression.[25]

In substance, Reid believed that the risk of war in the coming decade was relatively low. Nevertheless, the risk was quite real. The danger, he argued, arose not only from the expansionist policies of the USSR, but also – and this was what distinguished him from most of his colleagues – from those of the United States. In this context, Canada faced three separate yet interrelated problems. First, Soviet policies constituted a threat to the security of the West, and hence to Canada. Canada thus really had little choice but to side with the United States, which was the only country capable of opposing the USSR. Second, Canada had to try to dissuade American leaders from adopting too aggressive a stance toward Moscow. In other words, Canada had to try to contain not only the Soviets, but also the Americans! The third problem arose from the preceding two. To contribute to the defence of the West and to hope to influence Washington, Canada had to strengthen its military co-operation with the United States. But as wartime experience had shown, such close relations could lead to a reduction in Canadian sovereignty. While Reid recommended improving the North American defence apparatus, he also sounded a cautionary note:

Canada is being brought into still greater dependence upon the United States ... In the event of war we shall have no freedom of action in any matter which the United States Government considers essential ... In peacetime our freedom of action will be limited but it will not be non-existent. It will still be open to us to oppose the United States on certain issues in United States–Soviet relations ... The weight of the influence the Canadian Government can bring to bear on Washington is considerable. If we play our cards well we can exert an influence at Washington out of all proportion to the relative importance of our strength in war compared with that of the United States.[26]

It was in the balance of power that Reid found a common solution to these three problems. He proposed creating a new regional security organization "in which there would be no veto and in which each state would undertake to pool all its economic and military forces with those of the other members if any power should be found to have committed aggression against any member." According to Reid, a balance of forces would have a deterrent effect on the Soviet leadership, which he perceived as both cautious and calculating. Forming an alliance would therefore seem an appropriate means of achieving this end. "The balance of power against the Soviet Union would be greatly increased if the nations of the Western world were, for example, to organize in advance an alliance which would become immediately effective if the Soviet Union should commit aggression."[27]

The solution to the other problems – those posed by the United States – would flow naturally from this one. In parallel with the idea of a balance of power applied at the global level, the idea of a balance operating at the regional level emerged. To guarantee respect for Canadian sovereignty, and to have even the smallest chance of influencing Washington's policies, Canada had to promote a multilateral alliance between the United States and the countries of Western Europe. Within this framework, Canadians and Europeans could, if necessary, form a common front against unilateral decisions by Washington and exert concerted pressure on the American leadership.

Some authors have seen this reasoning as an indication of the essentially "realist" nature of Reid's approach. In fact, the main thing that it illustrates is the duality of his vision. For to contain the United States, Reid relied not only on power relationships within the alliance, but also, and more importantly, on the institutional rules that must structure relations between the future allies. Pushing this logic to the extreme, he proposed to create not a simple alliance, but a genuine federation of states. The "North Atlantic community," as Reid envisioned it, never came to pass, and article 2 of the Washington Treaty, which called for the alliance to cooperate on economic and social matters, is only a pale reflection of Reid's original plans.[28]

The proposed "federation" came a-cropper not only because of resistance on the part of the allies; it was also rejected by the Ottawa foreign policy bureaucracy. Reid hardly helped his cause with his own colleagues, who were finding his forceful efforts to advance his ideas increasingly annoying. Among those whom he alienated were Hume Wrong, A.D.P. Heeney, and Norman Robertson. At one point Wrong, Canada's ambassador to Washington, pointedly reminded Reid that "we are not establishing a federation but an alliance."[29] By the fall of 1948 relations between Wrong and Reid had become so poor that Reid asked Pearson and St Laurent to review his proposals and bring them to cabinet.[30] Heeney increasingly objected to Reid's tendency to harass senior officials and ministers, especially Pearson, on matters of even trivial significance.[31] As for Robertson, Reid's demeanour smacked of too many "remaining echoes from the Anglican prayer book."[32] Granatstein is surely correct in observing that Reid's growing unpopularity had much to do with the fact that he was never offered the job of under-secretary of state for external affairs.[33]

But if the concept of a "community" has been almost entirely forgotten, the metaphor of the counterweight has become an intrinsic element of Canada's strategic culture. Indeed, after 1948 the counterweight metaphor emerged as a touchstone and a common rationale in the discourse of the Canadian leaders and diplomats who were involved in creating the North Atlantic Alliance. This motivation was, moreover, mentioned explicitly by the Canadian representatives who participated in the forming of this new institution.[34] Reid returned to this idea himself during the period when the treaty was being negotiated[35] and in the years that followed. In April 1951, for instance, he wrote:

It has become increasingly apparent during the past year that one of the most difficult and continuing problems which Canada has to face is her relationship with the United States. While the problems for Canada are peculiarly difficult, all the other countries in the Western world are faced with the problem created by the fact that in a two-power world the United States is so much the preponderant power on our side. If there is a war and we win, it is highly probable that that part of the world which is not reduced to anarchy will be ruled pretty directly by the United States. If we have a long period of one-quarter or one-half war, there will be a strong tendency for the Free World to move in this direction of an American empire. One way in which this tendency may be resisted, perhaps successfully, is for the Free World to become increasingly subject to some sort of common constitutional structure ... Even in its present state, the North Atlantic Treaty Organization does provide a check and balance on United States power.[36]

Through the creation of the Atlantic Alliance, the counterweight metaphor has become one of the best-established images in the historiography of Canadian foreign policy.

The Counterweight as a Component of Canadian Strategic Culture

The counterweight metaphor fits neatly into the concept of strategic culture: this metaphor persisted, long after the original conditions that gave rise to it disappeared, and it still helps to guide Canadian strategic thinking and decision-making. In the literature it is inextricably linked with the other concepts used to describe and analyse Canadian foreign policy, including multilateralism, internationalism, and to a lesser extent, the notion of Canada as a middle power. Indeed, academics have been quick to adopt and use this metaphor in analysing Canada's reasons for joining the Atlantic Alliance in 1949.[37] Moreover, it has been employed in many articles and books on Canadian participation in security institutions and on defence policy in general.[38] Some authors have even attempted to isolate this factor and place it at the centre of their analysis.[39] The counterweight argument has also been cited in some debates with a prescriptive flavour. Most of those who have argued that Canada should continue its contribution to NATO (or else find itself marginalized in North America) have referred to it. This was the case, for instance, during the debates that preceded and followed the withdrawal of Canadian forces from Europe in 1992.[40] Thus, from its beginnings as a policy orientation, the counterweight metaphor became first a factor that *explained* the broad orientations of Canadian foreign policy, and then a *prescriptive* argument.

However, there were problems with the counterweight strategy. First, it was not clear – given the ambiguous (not to say metaphysical) nature of political balancing – whether there could be any knowable consequences of the strategy. How could one be certain that a counterweight effect was stemming from a counterweight strategy, when the dependent variable was so difficult to define and measure? Furthermore, does this metaphor really explain anything? And does it really constitute a guide for political action? The Atlantic Alliance did perhaps help to solve two of the three problems that Reid identified in his August 1947 memorandum: containing the Soviets and calming the bellicose instincts of the United States. But what of the third: enabling Canada to escape America's pull and preserve the sovereignty that was threatened by excessively close military co-operation? To answer this question, we must try to measure what impact the creation of the Atlantic Alliance has had on Canada-US bilateral relations. More precisely, we must determine whether the formation of NATO allowed matters that had previously been handled on a bilateral basis to be shifted to the multilateral sphere, and consequently, whether the new institution did in fact enable Ottawa to avoid an exclusive dialogue with the United States.

A review of the available archival documents reveals a fairly strict compartmentalization between bilateral and multilateral activities. This separation has satisfied Washington's desire to prevent its European allies from interfering in the management of the systems for defending US soil (and later, in the control of the apparatus of nuclear deterrence). But more curiously, it has satisfied some Canadian desires as well. It is significant that the Canadian diplomats involved in the negotiations in 1948 and 1949 that led to the creation of NATO rarely alluded to the defence of North America or to co-operation with the United States. Indeed, in 1948 one of the reasons favouring the creation of a new institution rather than an expansion of the Brussels Treaty was that the obligations under this treaty were not compatible with existing Canada-US agreements.[41]

It is clear that during the negotiations for the North Atlantic Alliance, Canadian policy-makers readily advanced the notion of a counterweight. Reid raised the possibility of transferring some of the activities involved in defending North America to a multilateral defence organization as an argument for Canada's participating in the alliance. "[U]nder such a treaty the joint planning of the defence of North America would fall into place as part of a larger whole and the difficulties arising in Canada from the fear of invasion of Canadian sovereignty by the United States would be diminished," he wrote in June 1948. "An Atlantic treaty would go a long way towards lessening the political difficulties of defence planning in Canada by bringing the United Kingdom, the United States and Canada into partnership."[42]

Along the same lines, Hume Wrong, Canada's ambassador in Washington and its principal negotiator for the North Atlantic Treaty, wrote to the secretary of state for external affairs, Lester B. Pearson: "If an Agreement on the lines that were discussed becomes reality, even though the parties might only be the United Kingdom, the United States, Canada and perhaps France and the Low Countries, it should considerably ease our problems in handling defence relations with the United States. [...] Our own political difficulties about permitting U.S. Forces to conduct certain operations or maintain certain facilities within Canadian territory ought to be substantially diminished if such activities could be seen as a fraction of a larger scheme."[43] However, beyond these general statements few concrete efforts were made to ensure that bilateral defence issues would henceforth be brought within the framework of NATO.

The opportunity to translate this plan into action did, however, arise in 1949 when NATO created five "regional strategic groups" to prepare operational plans for the zones covered by the alliance. One of these groups was the Canada–United States Regional Planning Group (CUS-RPG). As early as August 1949, when the discussions on the military structure of the Atlantic Alliance were getting under way, Pearson felt it unnecessary to create a Chiefs of Staff Committee for North America, like those created for the four other regional planning groups, largely because the existing mechanisms – the long-established Permanent Joint Board on Defence (PJBD) and the Military Cooperation Committee (MCC) – were working well.[44] However, in early 1950, Canadian diplomats began to consider the possibility of transferring the functions of the PJBD and the MCC to the CUSRPG. The American military refused, worried that this would allow the Europeans to interfere in the planning and direction of continental defence and consequently in the control of nuclear forces stationed on American soil. The Americans also feared that their European allies would demand the construction of an air-defence system comparable to that planned for North America. Finally, US authorities were worried that the CUSRPG, which reported to the NATO Military Council, might allow European allies too much access to secret information affecting the defence of North America. Sensitive to such arguments, the Canadian Chief of Staff, General Charles Foulkes, sided with the Americans, severely damaging Pearson's effort to link the defence of the two continents.[45]

Another opportunity to link North American and European defence arrangements arose in 1952, when NATO decided to convert the regional planning groups into "regional commands." Despite Canadian representations in favour of the idea, the CUSRPG was the only one of the five regional groups not converted to a regional command. The proposal was opposed by the American military, and it did not even garner the support of the Europeans, who had little desire to assume any responsibilities connected with the defence of North America.[46] Thus, in the early 1950s it became clear that, on the ground, the defence of Europe and that of North America would follow separate if parallel paths. The European counterweight – if there ever was one – did not save Canada from the vagaries of bilateral co-operation with the United States.

How can we explain why the Canadians did not push harder for a closer link between the defence of the two continents? The political scientist John Holmes offers one line of reasoning. Feeling the need to explain why Canadian diplomats did not try to shift bilateral issues into the framework of a multilateral institution, he argues as follows:

The principal reason for keeping continental relations in a separate compartment was probably Canadians' confidence in their ability to deal with the Americans. They did not entirely swallow the American assumption of being more virtuous than other countries, but there nevertheless was a belief in Canada that North American relations were conducted on a higher moral plane than those of other continents [...] Although they would never admit for a moment that Canadian-American relations were other than those between two sovereign countries, there was a tendency in Canada to think of these relations as their own private business in which outsiders, even an international organization, should not interfere.[47]

Though Holmes was referring to the UN, this comment is highly apposite to the Atlantic Alliance. Implicitly, Holmes was questioning whether there was even need to seek a counterweight!

Besides the creation of the Atlantic Alliance itself, perhaps the best known example of a policy that seems to have been directly inspired by the counterweight metaphor is the so-called "Third Option" strategy put forward by Pierre Trudeau's Liberal government in 1972. The strategy aimed to reduce American dominance of the Canadian economy through a trade diversification policy. Europe, naturally, was one of the main partners with which preferred trading ties were to be encouraged. In a White Paper on Canadian foreign policy toward Europe, published two years earlier, Europe was presented explicitly as a counterweight to American influence.[48] Moreover, as a study conducted in the mid-1970s on the image and policy preferences of the Canadian elite demonstrated, this idea was deeply rooted in the minds of Canada's senior public servants.[49] Paradoxically, Canada was promoting this economic policy at the very time it was substantially reducing its military contribution to the Atlantic Alliance. Indeed, Trudeau seems to have regarded NATO more as a burden that was distorting Canada's foreign and defence policies than a means of escaping the influence of the United States.[50] But by 1972–73 the Canadian government was already rediscovering the virtues of NATO as a tool for building a special relationship with its European allies, and in particular with the Federal Republic of Germany.[51] By the start of the 1980s, however, the failure of the Third Option had become obvious, marking the swan song of Canada's efforts to reduce the relative importance of its trade with the United States.

Despite the lack of any indication that there is, in fact, a viable counterweight across the Atlantic to which Canada can attach itself in order to avoid being absorbed by the United States, the quest for some kind of balance of power seems to have become a reflex among Canadian leaders. This reflex vividly illustrates how ideas can persist over time, even when the conditions that originally gave rise to them have disappeared, and how these ideas can influence policy development, even when there is no evidence that the resulting policies are effective. In that sense, this reflex bears witness to the existence of a strategic culture in Canada.

What explains the popularity and durability of the counterweight metaphor? Certainly part of the explanation is that it seems so simple and logical. Just like the theory of the balance of power that has fascinated so many international relations theorists since the eighteenth century, the counterweight metaphor owes its popularity to the fact that it seems to reflect simple common sense. Another part of the explanation – and this brings us back to the contribution of Escott Reid – is that this metaphor has generally been associated with idealist goals. The balance of power, as Canadians generally conceive it, does not result from a balance of *military* forces, but rather from the existence of international institutions where the rule of law and democratic principles prevail. Thus, a concept traditionally used by realists has come to be framed by an idealist logic.

Were Reid and His Contemporaries Liberal Realists?

In strictly theoretical terms Reid's ideas seem contradictory. How, after all, could any Kantian worth his salt be a realist, and vice versa? How can we reconcile Reid's apparent faith in the balance of power with his simultaneous belief in the ability of international institutions to moderate the impact of power relations?

There is a contradiction here only if we insist on rigidly compartmentalizing the "realist" and "idealist" schools of thought. It already becomes less disturbing when viewed from the standpoint of certain contemporary theories, such as defensive realism, constructivism, and neo-classical realism,[52] which, while accepting the realist axiom that power constitutes a key variable for understanding international relations, also agree that the ideas, perceptions, and values of the players involved contribute significantly to the explanation. But while the contradiction can be resolved by reference to current theories, this solution is unsatisfactory from a historical standpoint. How should we place Reid within the intellectual landscape of his times?

Perhaps if we were to permit ourselves recourse to the obsolete label of *liberal realist*, we might find a way to resolve the analytic tension in the various accounts of early Cold War Canadian foreign policy. For many, liberal realism must stand as the ultimate oxymoron, given that liberalism is said to be generative of a set of policy expectations decidedly at odds with those spawned by realism. Yet for an earlier generation of students of international relations – or at least of American foreign policy – liberal realism was a staple of discourse, deployed as if it actually meant something. Indeed, so familiar was the label that it was often simply taken to possess self-evident meaning. Any attempt to ascribe to it explicit content could result in a surprising characterization of it as an approach bearing hallmarks of what a later generation would come to call "critical theory." In the words of Robert W. Tucker, writing more than thirty years ago, liberal realism not only dominated the study of post-war American foreign policy, but it did so in a fashion that was "quite pervasively critical" of that policy.[53]

In this historiography, the American diplomatic record is marked by confusion over the ends and means of foreign policy, indeed, over the very nature and meaning of foreign policy. Given this general assessment, the question must arise: How did the United States nevertheless manage to do so well? For if the by now conventionally critical interpretation is correct, the fact remains that seldom, if ever, in history has ineptitude and misunderstanding paid off with such handsome results. It is this general theme that dominates the liberal-realist interpretation of American expansionism in the 20th century.[54]

Over the past three decades, and increasingly since the end of the Cold War, the notion of power creating "interests" has been attacked from a variety of perspectives, not least of which has been a constructivist emphasis upon identity as generative of interests. This, of course, is what Jeffrey Legro and Andrew Moravcsik were getting at in their obituary notice for realism,[55] though they expand the catchment area into which quondam realists have been carried beyond the constructivist (they call it "epistemic") basin and into the reservoirs of liberalism and institution-alism. Nevertheless, their critique is misplaced, for while relative power has always figured in realist accounts, it has never consistently been the only datum to have mattered, or even to have been the one to have mattered the most. James Kurth, for instance, holds it to be realism's "sense of tragedy and its resulting attitude of prudence" that has primarily set this approach apart from the others, and he may be right.[56]

What the liberal realists of an earlier generation added to the discussion was not so much their critical perspective but rather the thought that "ideals" did matter in American foreign policy, and by extension in international politics. They insisted, however, that idealism on its own needed always to be tempered by a prudent recognition of the realities attending the distribution of power and of threat. This was the message of one of Tucker's School of Advanced International Studies colleagues, Robert E. Osgood, whose major work on the radical reorientation of American foreign policy at mid-century bore the apt title, *Ideals and Self-Interest in America's Foreign Relations*.[57] For the liberal realists, "power" could not be the sole basis of policy-making, just as it could not constitute the sole variable in understanding policy; ideals also had their part, and it was by no means only the "idealists" who so argued.

It might be thought that liberal realism was a label developed by and for Americans. It might further be imagined that Canada has no realist tradition of which to speak, therefore any attempt to apply an American (and obsolete) label to the so-called "golden" generation of Canadian foreign policy-makers, the "Pearsonian internationalists" among whom few were as noteworthy as Reid, is bound to obscure far more than it could possibly reveal. To so argue would, however, be wrong.

It would be wrong because, in the first place, Canada *has* had a tradition of foreign policy analysis (and policy-making) that truly does deserve the label realist, even realism of a Waltzian nature, in which the system is primarily given its "structure" by the relative capabilities of the states composing it.[58] If realists, and here we mean the unalloyed, insist upon the centrality of relative power to foreign policy, then what label *should* we apply, if not "structural realists," to those legions of Canadian analysts (maybe even some policy-makers) who infer a distinct "role" for Canada stemming primarily if not exclusively from its (middle) power ranking? Though she abstained from so branding them, was not Maureen Appel Molot nevertheless correct in drawing our attention to the propensity of

Canada's political scientists to take their cues so diligently from assessments of relative capabilities?

Not only is the study (and practice) of foreign policy in Canada permeated by an unacknowledged structural-realism, but it also betrays evidence of having been propelled by some of the exact forms of prudentiality and calculation associated with a more traditional, "classical," variant of realism. Or at least it betrayed such evidence in the past, never more so than during the closing years of the Second World War and the early years of the Cold War. One should not confuse the internationalists of the golden age with those "idealists" imagined to be the polar opposites of the realists against whom they were pitted during the first "great debate" in international relations theory.

Was Reid one of these liberal realists? He gives every appearance of having been one, though he probably never used this label himself. But placing him within this intellectual tradition allows us not only to reconcile the apparent contradiction in his ideas, but also to see him as a product of his times and of the ideas that were then circulating.

What set the Atlanticist movement in train was a happy marriage of liberal-institutionalist idealism and the kind of realism that comes from having a clearly perceived great-power adversary. If ever there existed a "liberal-realist" security agenda, it can be glimpsed in the Atlantic vision of Reid, Pearson, and other leaders in Canada and elsewhere in the expanded North Atlantic triangle. Not all that was associated with Reid's realist side can be considered to have been "realistic" – witness the fate of the counterweight impulse in Canadian strategic culture. It remains to be seen whether Reid's "idealistic" side ultimately turns out to have a more enduring legacy, in light of the crisis facing Canadian diplomacy since the end of the Cold War.

NOTES

1 Non-Canadian authors tend to forget the contribution of Canadian diplomats to the development of NATO. This is particularly so in the United States, where the multilateralist movement that led to the creation of NATO is explicitly perceived as an "American one." See David G. Haglund, *The North Atlantic Triangle Revisited: Canadian Grand Strategy at Century's End* (Toronto: CIIA, 2000), 55–6.

Among Reid's many writings on the origins of NATO, are the following: "The Art of the Almost Impossible: Unwavering Canadian Support for the Emerging Atlantic Alliance" in André de Staerke, ed., *NATO's Anxious Birth: The Prophetic Vision of the 1940s* (New York: St Martin's Press, 1985), 76–86; "The Birth of the North Atlantic Alliance," *International Journal* 22 (Summer 1967), 426–40; "The Creation of the North Atlantic Alliance" in Jack L. Granatstein, ed., *Canadian Foreign Policy: Historical Readings* (Toronto: Copp Clark Pitman Ltd, 1986), 158–82; *Time of Fear and Hope: The Making of the North Atlantic Treaty, 1947–1949* (Toronto: McClelland and Stewart, 1977). See also John W. Holmes, *The Shaping of Peace: Canada and the Search for World Order, 1943–1957*, Volume 2, (Toronto: University of Toronto Press, 1982), 98–122.

2   Kim R. Nossal, *The Politics of Canadian Foreign Policy*, 3rd edition (Scarborough, Ont.: Prentice-Hall, 1997), 138–70; Peyton V. Lyon and David Leyton-Brown, "Image and Policy Preference: Canadian Élite Views on Relations with the United States," *International Journal* 32 (Summer 1977), 640–71; Haglund, *The North Atlantic Triangle Revisited*.

3   Colin S. Gray, "Strategic Culture as Context: The First Generation of Theory Strikes Back," *Review of International Studies* 25 (January 1999), 49–69.

4   Alastair Iain Johnston, "Thinking about Strategic Culture," *International Security* 19 (Spring 1995), 32–64, quote on 46.

5   Lowell Dittmer, "Political Culture and Political Symbolism," *World Politics* 29 (July 1977), 552–83, quote on 557–8.

6   Ibid., 568–9.

7   This duality is especially apparent in Greg Donaghy, ed., *Canada and the Early Cold War, 1943–1957* (Ottawa: Department of Foreign Affairs and International Trade, 1999); see articles by Denis Stairs, "Realists at Work: Canadian Policy Makers and the Politics of Transition from Hot War to Cold War" (91–116) and Stéphane Roussel, "L'instant kantien: la contribution canadienne à la création de la communauté nord-atlantique," 119–56. See also Stéphane Roussel, Paul Létourneau, and Roch Legault, "Le Canada et la sécurité européenne (1943–1952): À la recherche de l'équilibre des puissances," *Revue canadienne de défense* 23 (Summer 1994), 23–7; 24 (Fall 1994), 17–22. The duality of the policy pursued by Reid and his colleagues has been highlighted by Roger Epp, "On Justifying the Alliance: Canada, NATO and World Order" in Michael K. Hawes and Joel J. Sokolsky, eds, *North American Perspectives on European Security* (New York: Edwin Mellen, 1990), 89-121; and by David G. Haglund, *North Atlantic Triangle Revisited*, 21–9.

8 Quoted in Escott Reid, *Radical Mandarin: The Memoirs of Escott Reid* (Toronto: University of Toronto Press, 1989), 140.

9 Ibid.

10 Reid cited in Michael Horn, *The League for Social Reconstruction: Intellectual Origins of the Democratic Left in Canada, 1930–42* (Toronto: University of Toronto Press, 1980), 146.

11 J.L. Granatstein, in the present collection; Reid, *Radical Mandarin*, 122.

12 *A Programme of Immediate Canadian Action Drawn Up by a Group of Twenty Canadians*, Château Laurier, Ottawa, 17–18 July 1940, quoted in Claude Beauregard, "La coopération militaire et les relations canado-américaines vues par un groupe d'éminents canadiens en 1940," *Revue canadienne de défense* 21 (Summer 1992), 34. For another group of Canadians who were early critics of the United States, see J.L. Granatstein, "The Conservative Party and the Ogdensburg Agreement," *International Journal* 22 (Winter 1966–67), 73–6.

13 Norman Robertson, "Memorandum," 22 December 1941, reprinted in John Hilliker, ed., *Documents on Canadian External Relations* (hereafter DCER), *Volume 9: 1942–43* (Ottawa: Supply and Services Canada, 1980), 1125–31; H.L. Keenleyside, "Recent Trends in United States–Canada Relations," reprinted in *DCER* 9: 1131–6. These two documents are analyzed in Galen Roger Perras, *Franklin Roosevelt and the Origins of the Canadian-American Security Alliance, 1933–1945* (Westport: Praeger, 1998), 102–3; Denis Smith, *Diplomacy of Fear: Canada and the Cold War, 1941–1948* (Toronto: University of Toronto Press, 1988), 14–16.

14 On this subject, see Reid, *Radical Mandarin*; Smith, *Diplomacy of Fear*, 16–17.

15 Smith, *Diplomacy of Fear*, 16–17 ; J.L. Granatstein, *The Ottawa Men: The Civil Service Mandarins, 1935–1957* (Toronto: Oxford University Press, 1982), 245.

16 Quoted in Reid, *Radical Mandarin*, 158–9; and Smith, *Diplomacy of Fear*, 18–19.

17 Reid, "United States Policy Towards Canada," 29 February 1944, reprinted in John Hilliker, ed., *DCER*, *Volume 11: 1944–45 Part II* (Ottawa: Supply and Services Canada, 1990), 1400–05.

18 Quoted in Smith, *Diplomacy of Fear*, 22; and in Reid, *Radical Mandarin*, 160.

19 Although this metaphor was popularized by the writings of J.B. Brebner in the 1940s, according to Brian J.C. McKercher and Lawrence Aronsen, its origin dates back to the Imperial Conference of 1926. J. Bartlet Brebner, *North Atlantic Triangle: The Interplay of Canada, the United States and Great Britain* (New Haven, Conn.: Yale University Press, 1945); J. Bartlet Brebner,

"A Changing North Atlantic Triangle," *International Journal* 3 (Fall 1948), 309–19; B.J.C. McKercher and Lawrence Aronsen, "Introduction" in *The North Atlantic Triangle in a Changing World: Anglo-American-Canadian Relations, 1902–1956* (Toronto: University of Toronto Press, 1996), 4.

20 Haglund, *North Atlantic Triangle Revisited*, 22; Brebner, "A Changing North Atlantic Triangle," 318.

21 See the documents on this subject in Donald Page, ed., *DCER*, *Volume 12: 1946* (Ottawa: Supply and Services Canada, 1977), 1615–27.

22 Granatstein, *The Ottawa Men*, 248.

23 Escott Reid, "Political Appreciation of the Prospects of Soviet Aggression Against North America," 13 February 1947, reprinted in Norman Hillmer and Donald Page, eds, *DCER*, *Volume 13: 1947* (Ottawa: Canada Communication Group, 1993) 342–5; "Joint Intelligence Committee Strategic Appreciation," 15 March 1947, reprinted in *DCER* 13: 346–62; Minister in Switzerland to Secretary of State for External Relations, Despatch No G.1, 25 April 1947, reprinted in *DCER* 13: 363–7; George Kennan ("X"), "The Sources of Soviet Conduct," *Foreign Affairs* 23 (July 1947).

24 Escott Reid, "The United States and the Soviet Union: A Study of the Possibility of War and Some of the Implications for Canadian Policy," 30 August 1947, reprinted in Hillmer and Page, *DCER* 13: 367–82.

25 This idea was officially taken up by the Canadian government on 18 September in a speech that the secretary of state for external affairs, Louis St Laurent, gave at the UN. It is generally regarded as one of the first times that a Western leader endorsed this position. See C.P. Stacey, *Canada and the Age of Conflict: A History of Canadian External Policies, Vol. II: 1921–1948, The Mackenzie King Era* (Toronto: University of Toronto Press, 1981), 416.

26 Reid, "The United States and the Soviet Union," reprinted in Hillmer and Page, *DCER* 13: 380–1.

27 Ibid., 380. See also Reid, *Radical Mandarin*, 222–3; Reid, *Time of Fear and Hope*, 30-1.

28 Regarding the proposed "North Atlantic community," see Roussel, "L'instant kantien."

29 Ambassador in Washington to Secretary of State for External Affairs (SSEA), Telegram WA-2912, 12 November 1948, reprinted in Hector Mackenzie, ed., *DCER, Volume 14: 1948* (Ottawa: Canada Communication Group, 1994), 648.

30 Escott Reid, "Proposed Statement of Views of the Canadian Government on the North Atlantic Treaty," 15 November 1948, *DCER* 14: 664–5; Reid, "Draft Telegram (not sent)," 20 November 1948, *DCER* 14: 678–80. Lester B. Pearson, *Mike: The Memoirs of the Right Honorable Lester B. Pearson*, 3 vols (Toronto: University of Toronto Press, 1972–5), 2: 47 and 62. Wrong's increasing impatience with Reid's suggestions resurfaced in March 1949. See

Ambassador in Washington to SSEA, Telegram WA-834, 24 March 1949, reprinted in Hector Mackenzie, ed., *DCER, Volume 15: 1949* (Ottawa: Canada Communication Group, 1995), 595.

31 A.D.P. Heeney to Norman A. Robertson, 16 February 1949, file: Personal Correspondence, 1949–1952, MG 30 E163, NAC.

32 High Commission in the United Kingdom to SSEA (Robertson for Reid), 9 November 1948, reprinted in Mackenzie, ed., *DCER* 14: 641.

33 Granatstein, *The Ottawa Men*, 251–2.

34 See Roussel, Létourneau, and Legault, "Le Canada et la sécurité européenne."

35 Escott Reid raised this idea on several occasions. See, for example, "Canadian Attitude towards a North Atlantic Defence Agreement" (Draft), 26 June 1948 reprinted in Mackenzie, ed., *DCER* 14: 520–3; See also Reid, "Creation of the North Atlantic Alliance," 171.

36 Escott Reid, *Paper on Canadian Policy in NATO*, 28 April 1951, RG 25, Accession 90-91/008, Volume 26, NAC.

37 For example, see John English and Norman Hillmer, "Canada's Alliances," *Revue internationale d'histoire militaire* 54 (1982), 42; Tom Keating, *Canada and World Order: The Multilateralist Tradition in Canadian Foreign Policy* (Toronto: McClelland and Stewart, 1993), 83–92; Tom Keating and Larry Pratt, *Canada, NATO and the Bomb: The Western Alliance in Crisis* (Edmonton: Hurtig, 1988), 15–48; Paul Létourneau, "Les motivations originales du Canada lors de la création de l'OTAN (1948–1950)," in Paul Létourneau, ed., *Le Canada et l'OTAN après 40 ans, 1949–1989* (Québec: Centre québécois de relations internationales, 1992), 53–4; Albert Legault, "Trente ans de politique de défense canadienne" in Paul Painchaud, ed., *Le Canada et le Québec sur la scène internationale* (Québec: Presses de l'Université Laval – CQRI, 1977), 163; Joel J. Sokolsky, "A Seat at the Table: Canada and Its Alliances," in B.D. Hunt and R.G. Haycock, eds, *Canada's Defence: Perspectives on Policy in the Twentieth Century* (Toronto: Copp Clark Pitman, 1993), 149; Desmond Morton, "Defending the Indefensible: Some Historical Perspectives on Canadian Defence, 1867–1967," *International Journal* 42 (Autumn 1987), 636.

38 Paul Buteux, "Commitment or Retreat: Redefining the Canadian Role in the Alliance," *Canadian Defence Quarterly* 23 (December 1993), 12–16; André P. Donneur, "La fin de la guerre froide: le Canada et la sécurité européenne," *Études internationales* 23 (March 1992), 138; David Leyton-Brown, "Managing Canada–United States Relations in the Context of Multilateral Alliances" in Lauren McKinsey and Kim Richard Nossal, eds, *America's Alliances and Canadian-American Relations* (Toronto: Summerhill Press, 1988), 175–6; Roy Rempel, *Counterweights: The Failure of*

Canada's German and European Policy (1955–1995) (Montréal: McGill-Queen's University Press, 1996).

39 Nils Ørvik, "Canadian Security and 'Defence Against Help'," *Survival* 42 (January–February 1984), 26–31; Paul Létourneau, "Comment limiter un marché léonin?: Le Canada et le couplage stratégique avec l'Europe (1943–1952)," *XVII Congresso Internazionale di Storia Militare* (Rome: Commission internationale d'histoire militaire, 1993), 421–32.

40 For example, George Bell, "Whither Canada?: Long Term Strategic Requirements" in Alex Morrison, ed., *A Continuing Commitment: Canada and North Atlantic Security* (Toronto: CISS, 1992), 51; John Halstead, "Future Directions for the Alliance," *The Atlantic Council Letter* 3 (July 1992), 2; Brian MacDonald, *Minutes of Proceedings and Evidence of the Standing Committee on National Defence and Veterans Affairs* 13 (19 November 1991), 13; Stéphane Roussel, "Amère Amérique ... l'OTAN et l'intérêt national du Canada," *Revue canadienne de défense* 22 (February 1993), 35–42.

41 T.A. Stone, 28 July 1948, Mackenzie, ed., *DCER* 14: 546.

42 Escott Reid, *Memorandum for Mr Heeney*, 1 June 1948, RG 2, Vol. 112, dossier U-40-4, NAC.

43 Hume Wrong, 7 April 1948, Mackenzie, ed., *DCER* 14: 485–6.

44 Secretary of State for External Affairs to Ambassador in Washington, Telegram EX-2061, 24 August 1949, reprinted in Mackenzie, ed., *DCER* 15: 652.

45 William R. Willoughby, *The Joint Organizations of Canada and the United States* (Toronto: University of Toronto Press, 1979), 132–3; Holmes, *Shaping of Peace*, 278–9; Joseph T. Jockel, *No Boundaries Upstairs* (Vancouver: University of British Columbia Press, 1987), 96–7.

46 Willoughby, *Joint Organizations*, 133.

47 Holmes, *Shaping of Peace*, 252–3.

48 Government of Canada, Secretary of State for External Affairs, *Europe. Foreign Policy for Canadians* (Ottawa: Information Canada, 1970), 14–15.

49 Lyon and Leyton-Brown, "Image and Policy Preference," 650–3. The idea is, however, expressed implicitly: "The élite favours diminishing dependence upon the United States by increasing relations with third countries" (652).

50 Edna Keeble, "Rethinking the 1971 White Paper and Trudeau's Impact on Canadian Foreign Policy," *The American Review of Canadian Studies* 27, no. 4 (Winter 1997).

51 Charles Pentland, "L'option européenne du Canada dans les années '80," *Études internationales* 14 (March 1983), 39–58; Rempel, *Counterweights*; Michael J. Tucker, *Canadian Foreign Policy: Contemporary Issues and Themes* (Toronto: McGraw-Hill Ryerson, 1980), 127–8.

52 Gideon Rose, "Neoclassical Realism and Theories of Foreign Policy," *World Politics* 51 (October 1998), 144–72.

53   Robert W. Tucker, *The Radical Left and American Foreign Policy*, Washington Center of Foreign Policy Research: Studies in International Affairs 15 (Baltimore: Johns Hopkins Press, 1971), 21–2.

54   Ibid., 22–3.

55   Jeffrey W. Legro and Andrew Moravcsik, "Is Anybody Still a Realist?" *International Security* 24 (Fall 1999), 5–55.

56   James Kurth, "Inside the Cave: The Banality of I.R. Studies," *National Interest* 53 (Fall 1998), 34–45, quote at p. 45.

57   Robert E. Osgood, *Ideals and Self-Interest in America's Foreign Relations: The Great Transformation of the Twentieth Century* (Chicago: University of Chicago Press, Phoenix Books, 1964).

58   Kenneth N. Waltz, *Theory of International Politics* (Reading, Mass.: Addison-Wesley, 1979). Waltz writes, "[t]o define a structure requires ignoring how units relate with one another (how they interact) and concentrating on how they stand in relation to one another (how they are arranged or positioned)" (80).

"The Most Important Place in the World"

Escott Reid in India, 1952–57

GREG DONAGHY

Escott Reid's four and a half years in India were the most controversial period in his career. Since joining the Department of External Affairs in 1939, he had risen steadily through the ranks, becoming deputy under-secretary in March 1949. Although Reid had served a long spell that year as acting under-secretary, his boss, the secretary of state for external affairs, Lester B. Pearson, refused him the top post. That decision hurt, but Reid was comforted by Pearson's assurances that he would be considered again. Meanwhile, he told a friend, it was "essential that I go abroad soon to head a diplomatic mission in order to round out my training."[1] In the spring of 1952, Reid chose India as his finishing school and his proving ground.

Reid's choice reflected both his idealism and the razor sharp intellect that prompted J.L. Granatstein to describe him as "the mandarin who seemed to see the furthest ahead."[2] Reid went to India convinced that Western security during the Cold War depended not only on the West's ability to contain Communist expansion but more importantly on its capacity to resolve the growing tensions between "the white have nations and the coloured have-nots."[3] Good relations with India, the largest Asian democracy and an emerging voice for the developing world, seemed an essential Western prerequisite in this struggle for a new, more just, world order.

But Reid was also a tough-minded, professional diplomat who had worked hard to reach the highest levels in his department. In New Delhi, freed from Ottawa's daily diet of crisis after crisis, he found the time and distance he needed to discipline his idealism. During his first three years overseas, Reid waged a steady campaign to convince his minister to take a more active role in bridging the gulf that divided India from the West and its foremost power, the United States. His telegrams, letters and despatches offered thoughtful diagnoses and pragmatic solutions, winning him plenty of plaudits but few converts. Though he was sometimes frustrated by his inability to influence policy decisively, Reid visited Ottawa in the summer of 1955 confident of success. But the triumph he so badly wanted continued to elude him, and left him increasingly isolated in New Delhi on the eve of his most important test yet: handling India's reaction to the Hungarian and Suez crises that erupted in October 1956.

Escott Reid arrived in New Delhi in November 1952 just as an Indo-Canadian effort to advance the peace talks in Korea reached its climax at the UN. Alarmed by American plans to escalate the war if the deadlocked negotiations with China were not resolved, Pearson had thrown his complete support behind an Indian initiative to frame a compromise. Washington was outraged, but Pearson persisted and succeeded in bringing India and the US together for the first time on a major Korean initiative.[4] For Reid, who was soon shuttling back and forth through the streets of New Delhi with confidential messages for ministers and prime ministers, the experience was a heady introduction to the complexities of Indian diplomacy that delighted and amused him.[5]

The 1952 resolution confirmed Reid's view that there was indeed a "special relationship" between India and Canada. That relationship, he later argued in his book, *Envoy to Nehru*, was rooted in the new multiracial Commonwealth that developed once India, Pakistan, and Ceylon achieved their independence in 1947. As former British colonies, Canada and India shared a common political and cultural inheritance that made communication easy. Exposure to the Indian perspective on world affairs, particularly when presented by Jawaharlal Nehru, India's charismatic and persuasive prime minister, helped Ottawa develop a less rigid view of the Cold War world – a world many Americans divided simplistically into "them and us." The Indian influence was especially evident in Ottawa's take on the Cold War in Asia. Though Canada would never abandon its Cold War commitment to resist communist aggression, it was convinced that the job of containing Asian communism properly belonged to India. As historian Robert Bothwell put it so nicely, Indo-Canadian relations were to be "a marriage of Canadian [or Western] strategy with Indian tactics."[6]

But Pearson and Reid differed – and this difference would matter more as the decade progressed – over how far Canada should go to convince Washington to adopt New Delhi's more accommodating approach to relations with Moscow and Beijing. Pearson never shared Reid's unfettered enthusiasm for India or Nehru, whom he found difficult to handle and once described as "an extraordinary combination of a Hindu mystic ... and an Eton-Oxbridge type of Englishman."[7] Pearson was a realist, and he doubted Canada's capacity to influence India, which was, after all, a "Great Power."[8] More important, Pearson had served as ambassador in Washington, knew what the traffic would bear, and knew that relations with Washington mattered more than relations with Delhi. During the 1950 and 1951 UN debates over Korea, for instance, he had been careful to side with Washington rather than New Delhi when push came to shove. Canadian support for the 1952 Indian resolution was exceptional, and derived largely from the high stakes involved. David Johnson, Canada's ambassador to the UN, cautioned that "too much should not be made of Commonwealth solidarity on Korea [for] it was conditioned ... by the desire to put off ... any consideration of US proposals for the 'next stage' in Korea."[9] Pearson shared this view, and made sure that later Canadian efforts to interpret India to the US and vice-versa were carefully managed and strictly contained.

The limits that Pearson intended to impose on Canada's mediatory efforts were clear in the first major crisis that Reid confronted as high commissioner in the summer of 1953. With the Korean armistice in the offing, international attention shifted to the composition of the post-war political conference that the truce agreement envisaged for settling outstanding Asian issues. Canada favoured Indian membership for a variety of good reasons. India was the largest non-Communist power in Asia, with an immediate stake in the region's security. Its participation in the Korean conflict and its effort in 1952 to secure an armistice entitled her to a place at the table. Canadian officials also thought that Nehru would continue to interpret the Western point of view fairly to Beijing.[10]

Washington was sceptical and anxious to punish New Delhi for its often ambiguous posture toward the UN's role in Korea by denying India a place at the conference. Reid was alarmed and pointed out that a public humiliation of India would be "a terrible mistake, a frightful error; the effect on Indo-American relations would be deplorable." Ottawa must persuade Washington to change its mind.[11] Though Pearson shared Reid's fears, he made it clear that he was not "prepared to play the role of special advocate for India."[12] Indeed, when it was later decided to ask the UN General Assembly to assign India membership over American objections, Pearson left the running largely to the United Kingdom. He even refused to co-sponsor the necessary resolution until it became apparent that Canada was the only major Commonwealth nation *not* co-sponsoring the UN motion.[13]

Pearson was equally careful not to play too prominent a role in the next crisis in Indo-American relations: the US decision to conclude a military assistance agreement with Pakistan. When rumours of the pact spread in December 1953, Reid alerted Ottawa to the danger. He argued that in the short run the agreement would heighten tensions in the subcontinent, just as India and Pakistan seemed on the verge of resolving their bitter dispute over Kashmir. Nehru would be confirmed in his view that Eisenhower's foreign policy was dominated by "narrow military considerations," further reducing his willingness to cooperate with Washington and driving Indo-American relations to a new low. The agreement might even prompt some Indians to question the value of the Commonwealth connection if the United Kingdom, Australia, and Canada had no influence in a matter of such direct importance to two of their allies.[14]

Reid worried too about the long view. India was a country whose democratic development was threatened by the ferment of Hindu fundamentalism, industrial reaction, and Communism. Alone against these forces stood Nehru, whom Reid described as "a very great man ... liberal, humane, intelligent." Nehru was not perfect, to be sure, and Reid worried that his very greatness and pre-eminence among the Indian masses might tempt him to play the demagogue. If Indians came to believe that US military aid for Pakistan was intended to force India into closer alignment with the United States, Nehru might well feel compelled to respond with hostility. The result for the West would be disastrous.[15] Pearson was impressed and toyed with the idea of intervening in Washington.

Arnold Heeney, Canada's ambassador in Washington, hesitated. The US would resent the implication that its military assistance program might inflame international and sectarian tensions in Asia. This kind of argument would be "ill-received," and might spark a "violent reaction in the Congress and the press."[16] He challenged Reid's view that American policy seemed almost designed to provoke the Indian premier. Heeney was satisfied that the White House was well aware of Nehru's "value as a powerful moderate in an area where explosive forces lie so close beneath the surface." Moreover, the US administration doubted that Nehru would jeopardize the flow of American aid to India by reacting too strongly against American military aid to Pakistan. The United States was legitimately concerned with shoring up the Pakistan prime minister, who had impressed the White House as "a moderate and sincere man." Heeney dismissed fears that US military aid to Pakistan was intended to force India to embrace the United States as "far-fetched." Ultimately, he concluded, US military aid to Pakistan was designed to strengthen Western defences against Communism in South Asia and the Middle East.[17]

Pearson agreed. He was sceptical of Reid's fears about Hindu fundamentalism, which he thought "fell into [a] somewhat less ominous perspective when ... considered in relation to the broad pattern of world trends and, similarly, when ... viewed over the longer term in India itself." Pearson ignored his high commissioner's concerns about Nehru, whom he thought much tougher and more capable of handling India's competing domestic pressures than Reid acknowledged. The real issue was the immediate global struggle between the West and Communism. In this context, Pearson wrote Reid, American military aid for Pakistan is "in itself and within its limits ... not altogether a bad thing, especially when viewed in relation to forces at work elsewhere."[18]

If Ottawa hesitated to intervene in Washington on behalf of New Delhi, it was nonetheless ready to intervene in New Delhi on behalf of Washington. In March of 1954, Prime Minister Louis St Laurent arrived in India to "allay some of the more extreme fears of Western policy, and in particular of US policy, which preys on the minds of Indian leaders."[19] Reid was doubtful, but in the end, he felt that St Laurent had scored a small diplomatic coup. The prime minister gamely defended US policy in the Indian Parliament, before winning over the Indian press corps by spontaneously endorsing Nehru's call for a ceasefire in Indochina. After an uncertain start, St Laurent and Nehru had several frank and very friendly talks. Reid was delighted at this new evidence of a special relationship. He speculated that Nehru was drawn to St Laurent because the Canadian was "humble and modest and sincere." In turn, the Canadian prime minister was attracted by the way "in which Mr. Nehru feels himself as an agent or actor in the great drama of Indian history." Reid added: "Mr. St. Laurent is probably also as fascinated as other observers by the enigma of Mr. Nehru's mercurial temperament, the boyish enthusiasms, the restless energy, his genuine love and respect for the Indian peasant, his aristocratic temper, the touch of what Charles Ritchie calls the 'high Bloomsbury,' and behind it all, a sad, lonely face." In sum, Reid concluded, the visit was "an immense success and a personal triumph for Mr. St Laurent."[20]

Others were not so sure. Diplomat Charles Ritchie, who accompanied the prime minister to India, thought him put off – not attracted – by Nehru's Bloomsbury style. Nehru's lover, Lady Mountbatten, "struck a Mayfair note which the [Canadian] Prime Minister could not pick up."[21] Ritchie cautioned Reid against overemphasizing the St Laurent–Nehru axis. The Canadian prime minister was upset to learn that his Indian counterpart ordered American members of a UN observation team out of Kashmir in retaliation for Washington's decision to give US military aid to Pakistan. This attitude, he thought, "was unworthy of a statesman."[22]

Ritchie was also inclined to discount the impact of St Laurent's public appearances on India's relations with the West. The deputy under-secretary was dismayed by the anti-Americanism he encountered everywhere in India and hurt by the lukewarm reception accorded the prime minister's major speech. "I don't believe," he wrote in his diary, "that, apart from the meetings with political leaders, anything we have said or done on this visit has got across to the minds or hearts of these people. They are easily bored and I think they have been."[23] Indeed, they were more than bored, they were irritated. On his return to Ottawa, Ritchie was invited to the Indian High Commission for tea. The high commissioner referred to St Laurent's "accolade" to the US, and suggested that it "had produced an unfortunate impression ... that the Prime Minister was in some fashion acting as an emissary for the United States in making these remarks."[24]

Comments like these reinforced Pearson's determination not to get caught in the middle as relations between Washington and New Delhi grew worse in the spring and summer of 1954. The secretary of state for external affairs remained convinced of the important role India could play in settling Far Eastern issues, but was more careful than ever not to promote New Delhi too openly. At the Geneva Conference on Korea and Indochina, for instance, he made all the right noises about the need for Indian participation and encouraged the British foreign secretary, Anthony Eden, to take Nehru into his confidence. At the same time, he cautioned his officials that "he did not wish [Canada] to become the principal channel for informing the Asians of what took place at Geneva."[25] When he left the conference, which had failed to make much progress, Pearson maintained a similarly low profile. He quietly proposed a Commonwealth foreign ministers meeting to associate India more closely with Asian security arrangements. However, he insisted that India issue the invitations lest Washington, whose attitude toward India was now "almost pathological," learn of his involvement. When the press heard of the Canadian initiative, Pearson quickly retreated.[26]

Whatever his frustrations about Canadian and Western policy toward India, Reid kept them carefully in check. Self-aware and sometimes introspective, he had arrived in New Delhi conscious of his besetting sins of too much work, too much paper, and too much emotion. He worked hard to overcome them. The effort and its success were noted in the summer of 1954 by his good friend, Norman Smith, the longtime editor of the *Ottawa Journal*. "I've heard many good reports of Escott's work lately," he wrote, "and also that he is 'containing' his ardency! Dear God," he added, "why do the wise and the zealous have also to be thin and given to nerves whereas the great stupid dolts are all built like giants and feed on liquor and cheese?"[27]

But Reid soon allowed some of that "ardency" to show. Over the summer of 1954, he had become increasingly alarmed at the speedy collapse of Indo-American relations that followed the US decision to send military aid to Pakistan. Relations were further eroded by the American refusal to allow India to attend the Geneva Conference, and Nehru's overtures to Beijing and Moscow. In Indochina, where India and Canada were both members of the international control commissions overseeing the Geneva Accords, Reid suspected that India would soon come into direct conflict with the US, with unhappy consequences for Canada. Some immediate action was required. In three carefully argued and tightly written despatches sent to Ottawa in November and December

1954, the high commissioner set out to examine why India's relations with the West had soured, and what practical steps might be taken to restore them.

Reid's first lesson took as its theme the deterioration of relations between India and the United States. The root causes he summarized neatly under "the three 'C's': China, Colonialism and Communism." The US, he began, believed that Soviet and Chinese communism posed a real danger of aggression that could only be met successfully with the threat of collective action. India, on the other hand, thought that the US exaggerated this threat, and was suspicious that Washington's emphasis on bases, alliances, and armaments heralded the arrival of a new form of imperialism. This basic difference over the nature of communism had led inevitably to conflicts and disagreements over a host of issues since 1950: the legitimacy of the Beijing and Formosa governments, the Korean War, military alliances in Asia, US military aid for Pakistan, and even US aid to India.[28]

As he often did, Reid went back to first principles for his answers, and in his second treatise, he set out to explain the basic consideration behind India's foreign policy. New Delhi's approach to international affairs was rooted in the "hopes and aspirations" liberated during India's recent struggle for independence. As Reid recognized forcefully in many of his despatches from India, crushing poverty defined the new country. Justifiably preoccupied with its internal development, India could not maintain or improve its standard of living while responding to external threats through military strength. India could choose to rely on other states to guarantee its security, but that would effectively involve an alliance with one of the world's two opposing coalitions. This carried two unacceptable risks for India. First, alignment would further harden divisions in Asia and increase the danger of war on India's doorstep. Second, alignment would reduce India's capacity to follow an independent "national" foreign policy and would invite "subversive factions" to undermine Indian unity.

Reid was confident that Nehru would be able to contain this threat to India's national unity. He was less sure about the threat to Indian stability that arose from its gut-wrenching poverty. If this was left unchecked, internal forces would eventually destroy Indian democracy. Reid clearly accepted New Delhi's argument that it was in Indian and Western interests for India to harbour its scarce resources through a policy of non-alignment in order to devote them to the struggle against "poverty, illiteracy and disease." Indeed, he carried the argument one step further. Left to its own devices, India would probably tend to challenge China directly for the leadership of Asia. This explained, thought Reid, Indian resentment at US efforts to build defensive alliances in Asia, which reduced the number of non-aligned, potential allies that India could draw on in its competition with China. It also accounted in part for India's irritating determination to be a leading voice in the struggle against colonialism and racial discrimination, two issues on which most Asians were united.

Reid acknowledged that India's determination to remain non-aligned and neutral was likely to give rise to differences with the West, which the Soviet Union and China were beginning to exploit. But India was not yet lost. The more India drew China into Asia and forced it to become "Asia-minded," the weaker the link between Moscow and Beijing, and the more likely that China would follow a policy "consonant with the special pattern of [its] traditions." Moreover, Reid reminded his audience, India's government and judicial system were profoundly shaped by Western liberal democratic values, providing a basis for close cooperation between India and the West. And finally, there was Nehru himself: the son of an anglicized family, the Cambridge-educated Indian premier was a committed democrat who remained "subject to the influence of wise and patient counsel on the part of Western statesmen."[29]

Much would be accomplished, Reid argued in his third installment, if American diplomacy just tried to remove the feeling that Washington has simply written India off. It could easily follow the British example, and ask India for its views on Asian security, while keeping New Delhi informed about its own thinking. Without changing its policy in Asia, the United States could also acknowledge that a close relationship between India and China was helpful to the West. Further, Washington might be more understanding of the potential benefits of closer cooperation by the non-aligned powers in Asia. "None of these things," Reid pointed out, "require any change in United States foreign policy. They require merely changes in US diplomacy."[30]

This was Reid at his very best. Pearson was delighted and assured him that if "I could get [US secretary of state] Dulles alone, relaxed before a cheerful fire, and soothed by a glass of bourbon, I would read every word to him!"[31] But Washington dismissed Reid's despatches, fueling concern in Ottawa about the growing gulf that divided East from West. This concern accounted in part for the warm welcome accorded the March 1955 proposal that Canada supply India with an experimental nuclear reactor.[32] It also prompted Pearson, at long last, to intervene more directly in Indo-American affairs. In April, he decided to invite Nehru to Ottawa in hope of inspiring an invitation to Washington, which would, he thought, "provide the Americans with an opportunity to mend a few of their fences with the Indians without getting us involved."[33]

Reid had hoped for something a little grander, something with a little more vision. In early July 1955, refreshed by a holiday and buoyed by the warm reception that greeted a public lecture in Toronto on India's relations with the West, Reid headed to Ottawa to meet with Canadian policy-makers. Their discussion centred on a second set of recommendations for improving India's relations with the West that Reid had sent to Ottawa just before taking home leave in April. There were many things that Canada and its allies could do to demonstrate the importance they attached to India, but what Reid really wanted was a dramatic shift in Western aid policy. He hoped Canada might inspire it.

Reid had explored the theme several times since 1953, and his views were well known in Ottawa. India would retain a modern, democratic form of government only as long as its leaders were successful in their struggle against "poverty, sickness and illiteracy." Success depended on access to adequate foreign exchange for the next five year plan, a requirement estimated to total somewhere around a billion dollars. Reid put Canada's share at $250 million, a quadrupling of Canadian foreign aid. It was obvious that neither Canada nor the other leading Western donors would simply give this money to India. Nor would this be good. Many Indians resented the undignified haggling and surveillance from outside associated with foreign aid, and would much prefer to receive a low interest loan. A line of credit modelled on Canada's generous post-war loan to Britain would soothe Indian sensitivities, while allowing New Delhi to draw freely on the foreign exchange needed to sustain its economic growth.[34]

Reid was disappointed by his reception in Ottawa. Economic experts were generally sceptical of his case for long-term credits. They doubted that the government was ready to increase its economic aid substantially, and thought that loans ought to be left to the private sector or to international agencies such as the World Bank. More disturbing, there were some in Ottawa who even questioned Reid's basic political rationale for helping India. Their spokesman was Marcel Cadieux. Tough, forthright, and a devout Catholic, Cadieux had just returned from Vietnam, where he was involved in the frustrating struggle on the International Control Commission to get help for Catholics fleeing communist North Vietnam. Time after time, the Indian chairman had sided with the Polish delegate to deflect Canadian efforts. Cadieux pulled no punches. "There is," he began, "a misunderstanding between us and India on the subject of Communism, and I wonder whether this is not related to a more basic misunderstanding of the implications of the real nature of 'neutralism' as practiced by the Indians." In Cadieux's view, Indian neutrality or non-alignment was simply not compatible with fundamental Western moral values or interests.[35]

Cadieux's views were extreme. Nevertheless, they suggested a growing scepticism about India and Canada's relations with it that surprised and depressed Reid.[36] A quick trip to Washington, which Pearson and Heeney hoped would show the high commissioner how difficult it had become to influence US policy in Asia, added to Reid's frustration. He was especially distressed when the US assistant under secretary of state for Far Eastern affairs, the bombastic and simplistic Walter Robertson, dismissed the Beijing regime as being "as unrepresentative of China as [US Communist] William Z. Foster was of the United States."[37] Reid returned to New Delhi in the fall of 1955 in a glum frame of mind.

The high commissioner's mood was lightened in November, when Pearson stopped in India on his way home from the Soviet Union. The respite was short-lived. Pearson's talks with Nehru were frank and enjoyable, but he left Asia increasingly sceptical of India's non-aligned foreign policy. "People here are morbidly sensitive about their independent position, satisfied with, even proud about their 'neutralist' stand ... At times, this makes them unreasonable and self-righteous, as does their occasional assumption of superior virtue vis-a-vis the West."[38] The next month, when the two Soviet leaders, Nikita Khrushchev and Nikolai Bulganin, trolled through India, denouncing the West and scattering small dollops of aid to tremendous applause, Pearson lashed out at Nehru. To Reid's dismay, he publicly attacked Nehru for his lavish reception of the Soviet leaders and his failure to give "popular credit" to the US and its Western allies for their much larger economic aid program.[39]

Pearson was soon irritated with Reid himself. He was sceptical of Reid's efforts to downplay the long-term significance of the Khrushchev-Bulganin visit. He found Reid's overall conclusion – that there was no immediate cause for alarm – "far too complacent." He was particularly angry at Reid's offhand and unusually superficial description of the final Indo-Soviet communiqué as "a restrained document." Pearson insisted that in the circumstances of the visit, the joint communiqué's condemnation of military blocs "could only be interpreted as a condemnation of the Western bloc, and a clean bill for the Communists."[40]

In the face of the rebuke, Reid's spirits sank. Increasingly, he pinned his hopes on a possible new administration in Washington. "About all any of us can do now is to conduct a 'holding operation' for the next year," he wrote his children in December 1955, "to use whatever influence we have over the Indians to try to persuade them to refrain from saying and doing things which will irritate the West; and to do the same thing in reverse in Washington."[41] But the American elections were still far away, and before long, the Hungarian and Suez crises cast a deep pall over the international landscape, and over Escott Reid and his career.

The two crises showed Reid at his very worst. Still recovering from an attack of jaundice suffered during the summer of 1955, he was easily tired and depressed. When the crises erupted, he was swept away by a storm of competing emotions that he could still recall vividly when writing his memoirs some forty years later. "I was shaken by feelings of terror, pity and anger," he wrote, "pity for the people of Hungary, anger at the actions of the Soviet Union, Israel, Britain and France."[42]

Reid was alarmed by Nehru's decision to condemn the British and French effort to seize the Suez Canal from Egypt, while refusing to denounce the Soviet Union's actions in Hungary. This time the Western world would neither understand nor forgive Nehru for his double standard. At the same time, Reid felt that Nehru, once shown the error of his ways, would be so repelled by the Soviet Union's behavior that he would ally himself more closely than ever with the West. Reid immediately launched an unauthorized crusade for Nehru's loyalties.

As the two crises deepened in early November, Reid grew more anxious about the possibility of a world war. He bombarded Pearson in New York with a stream of increasingly feverish telegrams containing useless and gratuitous advice. In New Delhi, he continued his campaign to convince Nehru to condemn Soviet actions in Hungary. When the high commissioner heard on the evening of 4 November that Soviet troops had returned to Budapest to suppress the popular uprising, he immediately approached Rag Pillai, the secretary general of the Indian foreign ministry. During an emotional midnight encounter, Reid went on for almost an hour, conjuring up lurid and unlikely images of a world on the edge of Armageddon. He begged Pillai to convince Nehru to urge Moscow to retreat from Hungary. Pillai was doubtful, and suggested instead that Reid ask St Laurent to send a message to Nehru directly, confident that the Canadian premier would know what to say.[43]

Pillai's instincts were right. Ottawa's perspective differed from Reid's. St Laurent and Pearson were far more concerned with extracting Britain and France from the Middle East than with the situation in Hungary, where there was little the West could do, short of war, to restrain Moscow. When Nehru used a speech on 5 November to equate the situations in Hungary and Suez, St Laurent responded with a message to the Indian leader partly designed to avoid a bilateral showdown over Hungary. It was a helpful message that acknowledged their differences over events in Eastern Europe, but noted with satisfaction that Canada and India were working closely together in New York on a peacekeeping force for the Middle East.[44] Just in case Reid missed the point, Pearson cabled him that Nehru's statement "was perhaps all we could hope for." He added that "we should not ... press further at the risk of turning the Indians sour."[45]

Hoping for something that might influence the Indian position, Reid was disappointed with St Laurent's message, which he later described as "banal."[46] He dismissed Pearson's warning, which he received just as he was reading reports of Nehru's second, ambiguous speech on the Hungarian crisis. When Nehru described the events in Hungary as merely a "civil conflict," Reid was convinced that Canada would act and he renewed his drive to convert Nehru. Pearson was irritated. "The Minister, who is now in New York for the General Assembly," the Department informed Reid on 12 November, "considers that it would be unwise to continue the campaign on the Hungarian question any longer and requests that you should not take any further initiatives except on express instructions."[47] Reid was also rebuked the same day for placing too high a priority on his telegrams from India.

The messages, distributed widely, were a humiliation. Reid's longtime colleague and friend, Norman Robertson, protested strongly, reminding Pearson of Reid's value: "One of Escott's qualities which much of the time is a source of strength is his faculty for identifying himself unreservedly with the fortunes of the issue or the idea which is uppermost in his mind. This means that he sometimes overlooks things and needs pulling up, but I don't think he should ever be pulled down quite so severely as in these two telegrams. I think he has been doing a remarkably good job in India, and he probably wouldn't be doing such a good job if he did not believe it the most important place in the world."[48]

In any event, Pearson's rebuke was too late. Reid met with Nehru on 13 and 14 November, passing on to the Indian prime minister Canadian appreciations of the situation in Hungary and at the UN in New York. At the same time, he continued to swamp the Department with advice and suggestions for addressing both the short- and long-term consequences of the crisis. Jules Léger, the under-secretary of state for external affairs, sent a third and final message, urging Reid to contain his ardor. Though the wording was more sensitive and acknowledged Reid's contribution, the meaning was clear enough: "I have become anxious – and this anxiety is shared by all your friends here including the prime minister and minister – because of the extra burdens imposed upon you during this period of tense crisis. We must keep our heads cool even if we are tempted to reason with our hearts. You have already done much in this emergency but from now on you should concentrate on matters of direct and primary concern to Canadian-Indian relations."[49] Reid appealed directly to Pearson for help, but was met with silence.[50] His campaign for Nehru's allegiance was effectively over.

It is still unclear what impact Reid's efforts in New Delhi had on Nehru's evolving views towards the Soviet role in Hungary. Nehru's official biographer thought it "debatable" that Canada had "much to do" with Nehru's eventual decision to denounce Moscow's actions in suppressing the Hungarian Revolution.[51] Given the number and range of sources of pressure on Nehru during the crisis, this is probably a fair assessment. It is also unclear what impact the Hungarian and Suez crises had on Reid, and his future with the Department. His unrestrained and emotional reaction during the crises probably confirmed the Department's view that Reid lacked the *gravitas* required of its most senior officials. Reid's ambition to spend the rest of his working life as under-secretary, ambassador to Washington, and high commissioner in London was never fulfilled.[52]

Reid's accomplishments as high commissioner in India are also difficult to document and evaluate. During his four years in New Delhi, he repeatedly failed to convince his minister or his department to undertake the kind of dynamic, interpretative role between East and West or North and South that he thought Canada was capable of playing. Despite repeated efforts, he was unable to overcome Ottawa's reluctance to embark on a dramatic new aid venture, the central feature in his program for tying India to the West. Indeed, by the time he left New Delhi in the spring of 1957, there was a large pocket of anti-Indian sentiment spread throughout the Department, largely, but not exclusively, the product of ceaseless bilateral squabbles over the war in Indochina. But there was one real and very important success. Through his letters, telegrams, and despatches, Reid forcefully compelled Pearson and his officials to engage India, its problems and its perspectives. For Canada, Escott Reid put India on the map.

NOTES

1 Escott Reid to Dana Wilgress, 8 April 1952, Escott Reid Papers, Volume 37, National Archives of Canada (NAC).

2 J.L. Granatstein, *The Ottawa Men: The Civil Service Mandarins, 1935–1957* (Toronto: Oxford University Press, 1982), 237.

3 Escott Reid to Dana Wilgress, 8 April 1952, Escott Reid Papers, Volume 37, NAC.

4 Greg Donaghy, "Pacific Diplomacy: Canadian Statecraft and the Korean War, 1950–53," in Rick Guisso and Yong-Sik Yoo, eds, *Canada and Korea: Perspectives 2000* (Toronto: University of Toronto Press and the Centre for Korean Studies, 2001).

5 Escott Reid to L.B. Pearson, 21 January 1953, Pearson Papers, Volume 12, NAC.

6 Robert Bothwell, "Eyes West: Canada and the Cold War in Asia," in Greg Donaghy, ed., *Canada and the Early Cold War, 1943–1957* (Ottawa: Department of Foreign Affairs and International Trade, 1998), 65–6.

7 L.B. Pearson, *Mike: The Memoirs of the Right Honourable Lester B. Pearson, Volume 2, 1948–1957* (Toronto: University of Toronto Press, 1973), 118.

8 Escott Reid, Memorandum of Conversation with L.B. Pearson, 9 September 1952, Reid Papers, Volume 10, NAC.

9 Permanent Representative to the UN to SSEA, 31 December 1952, reprinted in Donald Barry, ed., *Documents on Canadian External Relations (DCER), Volume 18: 1952* (Ottawa: Supply and Services Canada, 1990), 468.

10 Ottawa to New York, Telegram No 424, 24 July 1953, reprinted in Donald Barry, ed., *DCER, Volume 19: 1953* (Ottawa: Supply and Services Canada, 1991), 130–2.

11 New Delhi to Ottawa, Telegram No 131, 4 July 1953 and New Delhi to Ottawa, Telegram 150, 20 July 1953, reprinted in *DCER* 19: 118, 127–8.

12 Ottawa to New Delhi, Telegram No 173, 6 August 1953, reprinted in *DCER* 19: 146.

13 New York to Ottawa, Telegram 5, 15 August 1953, reprinted in *DCER* 19: 163–4.

14 New Delhi to Ottawa, Telegram 303, 12 December 1953, DEA File 50317-40, NAC.

15 Escott Reid to L.B. Pearson, 23 December 1953, reprinted in Greg Donaghy, ed., *DCER, Volume 20: 1954* (Ottawa: Canada Communication Group, 1997), 919–20.

16 Washington to Ottawa, Telegram WA-2877, 18 December 1953, DEA File 50317-40, NAC.

17 A.D.P. Heeney to Escott Reid, 29 January 1954, Reid Papers, Volume 33, NAC.

18 L.B. Pearson to Escott Reid, 6 February 1954, Reid Papers, Volume 10, NAC.

19 Acting USSEA to Deputy USSEA, 2 February 1954, reprinted in Donaghy, *DCER* 20: 925–30.

20 Escott Reid to L.B. Pearson, 8 March 1954, reprinted in Donaghy, *DCER* 20: 935–40.

21 Charles Ritchie, *Diplomatic Passport: More Undiplomatic Diaries, 1946–62* (Toronto: Macmillan, 1981), 67.

22 Charles Ritchie to Escott Reid, 23 April 1954, Reid Papers, Volume 9, NAC. Ritchie's letter also included the following observation: "You know that the Prime Minister is hardly voluble on the subject of personalities, but I detected, I think, a distinct reservation in his later references to Mr. Nehru after the visit – and he expressed quite strong disapproval in talking to me – of Mr. Nehru's stand over the American UN Observers."

23 Ritchie, *Diplomatic Passport*, 67.

24 USSEA to High Commissioner in India, Letter No K-262, 12 April 1954, reprinted in Donaghy, *DCER* 20: 940–1.

25 J.A. Chapdelaine to John Holmes, 11 May 1954, reprinted in Donaghy, *DCER* 20: 1672–3.

26 L.B. Pearson to Escott Reid, 2 June 1954, and Ottawa to New Delhi, Telegram 198, 25 June 1954, Pearson Papers, Volume 12, NAC.

27 Norman Smith to Escott Reid, 1 August 1954, Escott Reid Papers, Volume 36, NAC.

28 High Commissioner in India to SSEA, Despatch No 1298, 11 November 1954, Pearson Papers, Volume 12, NAC.

29 High Commissioner in India to SSEA, Despatch No 1318, 18 November 1954, Pearson Papers, Volume 12, NAC.

30 High Commissioner in India to SSEA, Despatch 1377, 1 December 1954, Pearson Papers, Volume 12, NAC.

31 L.B. Pearson to Escott Reid, 23 December 1954, DEA File 50018-40, NAC.

32 For a fuller discussion of the motives behind the Canadian gift, see Greg Donaghy, "Nehru's Reactor: The Origins of Indo-Canadian Nuclear Cooperation, 1955–59," a paper prepared for the South Asian Studies Conference, Université Laval, Quebec City, 25–7 May 2001.

33 Jules Léger, Memorandum for the Minister, 2 May 1955, DEA File 50349-40, NAC.

34 High commissioner in India to SSEA, Despatch No 338, 28 March 1955, DEA File 9126-40, NAC.

35 Marcel Cadieux, Memorandum for File, 27 June 1955, DEA File 9126-40.

36 Reid, *Radical Mandarin*, 277.

37 Escott Reid to L.B. Pearson, 16 September 1956, Pearson Papers, Volume 12, NAC.

38 L.B. Pearson, Secret Journal of his Asian Trip, [November 1955], Reid Papers, Volume 9, NAC.

39 See Escott Reid, *Radical Mandarin*, 280.

40 L.B. Pearson to Escott Reid, 11 January 1956, Pearson Papers, Volume 12, NAC. The letter only discusses the United Kingdom High Commissioner's reports, but as Pearson and Reid both knew, Reid had sent similar assessments to Ottawa. For Reid's assessment of the Soviet communiqué, see New Delhi to Ottawa, Telegram No 866, 23 December 1955, Pearson Papers, Volume 52, NAC.

41 Escott Reid to Patrick Reid, 18 December 1955, Escott Reid Papers, Volume 21, NAC.

42 Escott Reid, *Radical Mandarin*, 282.

43 New Delhi to Ottawa, Telegram 670, 5 November 1956, Escott Reid Papers, Volume 8, NAC.

44 Ottawa to New Delhi (St Laurent to Nehru), Telegram KK-145, 7 November 1956, Reid Papers, Volume 8, NAC.

45 Ottawa to New Delhi, Telegram SS 251, 9 November 1956, Escott Reid Papers, Volume 9, NAC.

46 Escott Reid, *Hungary and Suez 1956: A View from New Delhi* (Oakville, Ont.: Mosaic Press, 1986), 70.

47 Reid reproduces this telegram in his letter of 19 November 1956 to L.B. Pearson, Pearson Papers, Volume 8, NAC.

48 Norman Robertson to L.B. Pearson, 13 November 1956, cited in Escott Reid, *Radical Mandarin*, 286.

49 Ottawa to New Delhi, Telegram G-635, 16 November 1956, Escott Reid Papers, Volume 8, NAC.

50 Escott Reid to L.B. Pearson, 19 November 1956, Pearson Papers, Volume 12, NAC.

51 S. Gopal, "The Halcyon Fifties," *The Book Review* (India), July–August 1981, 16.

52 In the early spring of 1957, to Reid's considerable disappointment, Pearson offered him the post of permanent representative to the United Nations. Prime Minister John Diefenbaker rescinded the appointment in the fall of that year, when Reid leaked word of his new posting to the press. See Jules Léger to Reid, 13 May 1957 and Reid to Léger, 22 May 1957 in Escott Reid Papers, Vol 28, NAC; Greg Donaghy interview with Tom Delworth, 22 March 2003.

5 The Radical Banker

Escott Reid, the World Bank, and Aid to India, 1962–65

BRUCE MUIRHEAD

Escott Reid arrived at the International Bank for Reconstruction and Development (IBRD) or – as it's more commonly known, the World Bank – in July 1962. He was fifty-seven years old and had spent most of his career with Canada's small, liberal Department of External Affairs. It was a difficult change to make. At the World Bank's headquarters in Washington, he encountered an intensely conservative bureaucracy whose guiding philosophy clashed with his own social democratic beliefs. Even so, the Bank provided some scope for Reid's talents. The early 1960s was an important time for the Bank and for its foreign aid activities in India and Pakistan, which Reid managed as the new director of the South Asia and Middle East Department (SAMED). By 1962, with its aid program in South Asia beginning to stagnate in the face of India's often inefficient and corrupt bureaucracy, the Bank resolved to make its efforts more productive. At the same time, India's economic policy-makers – shaken from their lethergy by communist China's surprising victory over India in the 1962 border war and then by Nehru's death in 1964 – were more open to change than ever before. The circumstances provided Reid with an ideal opportunity to shape Bank policies at headquarters in Washington and in India, a country he loved dearly. He set out in July 1962 to modernize the World Bank's administrative procedures and convince it to help the small farmer on a tiny parcel of land. In short, he was determined to usher his employer and its clients into the 1960s.

Escott Reid was an Indophile who had served as Canada's high commissioner in India from 1952 to 1957. A vocal advocate of increased economic aid to India, he maintained an active interest in that country's economic development even after he left New Delhi, enjoying a growing international reputation as an aid expert. In 1959 Senator John F. Kennedy even suggested appointing him to a high-profile mission of donor countries investigating economic conditions in the subcontinent. Although Reid was not chosen for the job, he was asked to comment on the final report, and his lengthy memorandum was circulated widely within the World Bank and passed on to Indian Prime Minister Jawaharlal Nehru in January 1961. It was hardly surprising that Eugene Black, president of the IBRD, should ask Reid to join the Bank in January 1962.

Black wanted to make Reid "a Consultant ... at a very senior level to undertake special assignments as they arise." He explained to the Canadian diplomat that the Bank's "experience indicates that we are almost continuously involved in delicate and important negotiations of one type or another ... which can only be handled by a member of the management or by a senior-level consultant of your stature."[1] With its promise of considerable professional autonomy, this was an attractive proposition that Reid could not easily pass up. He was unhappy with his current posting as ambassador to West Germany, with whom Canada's relations were largely routine and uneventful. As Douglas Small, a former colleague, recalled "Reid was out of sync and out of sorts with Ottawa while in Bonn. He was losing his audience ... and he knew it."[2] He would have preferred to be either under-secretary of state for external affairs or ambassador in Washington but neither post was up for grabs.[3] He leapt at Black's offer.

Reid's new job got off to a rocky start. By the time he joined the bank in July 1962, Black had decided to retire. Worried that his successor might not continue to use free-ranging consultants, leaving Reid without a real assignment, he appointed Reid head of the South Asia and Middle East Department, the largest one at the IBRD.[4] This was indeed farsighted of Black. The new president, George Woods, appointed on 1 January 1963, was not much interested in Reid or his special missions. Woods was an abrasive, "unpolished" personality, who "criticized staff harshly and publicly, and argued with, rather than pacified, his Executive Board."[5] He took an early opportunity to suggest to Reid that the Canadian diplomat might be happier heading the Western Hemisphere Department, a demotion that Reid resisted.[6]

Despite this uncertain beginning, Reid's new department was interesting. It consumed roughly 35 percent of the IBRD's total loan portfolio and was easily the most significant department at the Bank, with a staff of seventeen "first class officers." As Reid settled in, he spent the first six weeks on the job learning about "some of the problems of the Bank."[7] He quickly concluded "that the question which lies at the root of most discussions in the Bank is whether the Bank is exerting to the full and in the wisest possible way the influence over the policies of underdeveloped countries which it derives from its reputation and from its ability to give or refuse loans and credits." Though Reid was sensitive to the needs and aspirations of developing countries, and wrote at length on the need to remove the "impression that the Bank is an Anglo-American institution," he clearly thought that the Bank was not doing enough to make its beneficent influence felt among its client states.

This was especially true of the Bank's role in India, where Reid returned for a visit in early 1963. This was an important trip for the new SAMED director. Much of the Bank's credibility and cash was tied up in Indian projects, and one of the more important jobs that Reid would undertake would be to attend the Aid-India consortium meetings, usually held four times per year. The establishment in 1958 of the aid consortium for India, which counted among its members Canada, France, Japan, the United Kingdom, the United States, and West Germany, represented a new way of disbursing World Bank assistance. India, the globe's largest democracy and the foil to the example presented by another Asian power, the Communist People's Republic of China, was considered a special prize.[8] The consortium was, according to Ashoka Mehta, the Indian minister of planning, "a symphony orchestra of which the Bank was the conductor and the governments the members of the orchestra. The Indians did their best to provide the conductor with a good score."[9] Significantly for Reid, this score had recently changed and the Bank's role had become more important with the Chinese invasion of India in the fall of 1962. The Indian army was routed and the Communists had emerged from the conflict completely victorious, a disconcerting and disquieting development for Western interests in South Asia.

Despite a crowded and busy itinerary, Reid was excited by the chance to visit the country he had left six years earlier. He was pleased with the many basic physical improvements in Indian life that had been adopted in this short period. More important, as he told the Bank's senior administration in a memorandum (which Nehru read and commented on), he was struck by the influence of the recent Chinese invasion of India. The country was more united than ever before and a "healthy adjustment" was taking place in Indian foreign policy. There was, he wrote, "an increasing consciousness of the danger that in the next few years India may be ringed about by countries in the Russo-China bloc or subservient to that bloc: e.g. Burma, Laos, Cambodia, Viet Nam, Ceylon, Indonesia, Nepal."[10] India was concerned about that possibility, and its nervousness could only help the West in its effort to win over this key ally in the battle against international communism.

However, there were also some "discouraging" features on which Reid commented. This list included inefficient industrial and agricultural production, the continuing sterile debate (or so he thought) between the merits of capitalism and socialism, and the endemic corruption that plagued the lower levels of Indian government and society. Surprisingly for a social democrat, Reid was especially concerned that there was "not enough recognition by the Indian Government that in any society ... the rate of economic development will be unnecessarily slow if prices, profits, incentives and disincentives, rewards for success and penalties for failure, are not allowed to play an important role in both the public and private sectors. At present in India these factors are not permitted to play a suffi-ciently important role." In other words, "the market" should be allowed to play a larger role in the determination of price and profit.

Convincing India, even in the wake of its war with communist China, that New Delhi should allow for greater market discipline in its economy was no easy task. For instance, differences naturally arose over the nature of industrial development. Given its substantial commitment to India, the Bank believed it had a certain proprietary interest in Indian economic policy, which it hoped would encourage the flow of investment for private sector industrial development. On the other hand, the Indians, and in particular the minister of finance, T.T. Krishnamachari, were powerful proponents of the development of industry by the *public* sector. Both Eugene Black and George Woods felt this an abomination and were reluctant to use Bank assistance to further this objective. But the Indian position was also sometimes confusing and inconsistent. While they generally opposed the Bank on this issue, at times senior officials would indicate a willingness to study the Bank's position in preparation for reducing the country's restrictions on private development. Not surpris-ingly, this apparent "flexibility" was greeted with considerable scepticism both by field officers in close contact with the government and at IBRD headquarters.[11]

Preparing for consortium meetings took a good portion of Reid's time. The so-called pledging sessions were held once per year (although pressure would be applied at other times to encourage members to up the ante – Ben King, the Bank's resident representative in New Delhi, called this "the consortium abracadabra"), and it was always a chore to line up the necessary countries along with the amounts that they would dedicate to Indian aid.[12] There were also constant attempts to interest more countries in consortium membership to lessen the burden on those already participating, an exercise in which Reid participated regularly. Gratifyingly for Reid and his colleagues, with sufficient "abracadabra" the amounts pledged sometimes rose. During a fairly typical 1962 session, for example, Japan offered an additional US$15 million to its existing contribution, which was raised again some months later to US$20 million. The United States had also offered an additional US$500 million, but that money would only be forthcoming if it were matched by other's proportional commitments. And as Reid told Burke Knapp, a Bank vice-president, Congress was reluctant to move away from that policy.[13]

There were other problems with the Aid to India consortium, not least a growing dissatisfaction among the members with *how* the money was being spent. Ben King spoke to this point and the intensely bureaucratic nature of the Indian civil service in a letter to Reid. The Bank's New Delhi representative was "impressed with the need for a radical reform of economic policy and practice ... I come across instances of misuse of economic resources and perhaps human resources, too ... Bringing the reform about depends on exerting the right pressure at the right time – or rather, times."[14] King harshly criticized all the elements involved in India's development. The civil service he dismissed as "not geared to development problems," and "scared to death of decisions." Indian economic policy, he described as "hopelessly confused," with "no real overall policy-making body [or] mechanism capable of ascertaining fact and presenting issues squarely." He thought the results were "fragmentation, incoherence and superficiality of economic policy." The debilitating atmosphere prompted King to "wonder to what extent the image of India created in Washington has been influenced by the highly civilized personality of B.K. Nehru. I suspect that between the image and the reality there is a long shadow – and lots of shadow prices, too."[15]

Reid was sympathetic but he had no easy or elaborate solution. Drawing on his long service in Canada's foreign ministry, he advised King:

I know that you must find ... this whole business of how an institution like the Bank can exercise the maximum beneficial influence on the policies of the central and state governments of a country like India complex and fascinating. I find it interesting to compare this problem ... with the one I've spent so many years with ... how a country like Canada can exercise the maximum influence on countries like the United States, Great Britain and India.

Here the road to the palace of wisdom was the realization that success was not measured by the wisdom of the advice we gave but by how much of our wise advice was accepted. It often meant giving advice in the form of information. It usually meant putting the information and advice in at as many levels as possible from junior experts to prime minister and in such a way as to strengthen the hands of the "sensible people" in the government – i.e., the people who agreed with us. It meant not insulting the intelligence of our foreign colleagues by adding two and two, especially when the answer four was unpleasant. It meant a willingness to let the other country take credit for our bright ideas. It usually meant confining our complaints to matters in which there was a direct, immediate and important Canadian national interest.[16]

While Ben King, an American working in India, might not fully appreciate the advice, it was still a good description of what was required, and could perhaps be summed up in a word – patience.

But patience could only take one so far, and India's reputation as personified by Nehru had resulted in Western indulgence, which, as the eminent economist Jagdish Bhagwati later noted, allowed the country to "minimize the warts in her policies, exaggerate her performance and her potential, and also produce aid support."[17] But by late 1963, with almost US$2.37 billion in aid money washing around the subcontinent, and another US$1.25 billion on request for 1963, the question of injecting some rationality into the process had become a serious issue. While all could agree that there was "no simple answer to India's development problems,"[18] some consortium members were tired of pouring good money after bad, especially if the results were negligible. The Germans and the French tended toward that position and they did not want to continue "to put up more and more money without any indication of where the [Indian] economy [was] heading."[19] The result, at least according to Peter Wright, was that "the way things are going at present, the Indian Government is helping to discredit the image of foreign assistance through the developing world."

Equally serious was India's high level of debt racked up by years of multi-billion dollar borrowing. Only a relatively small proportion of that debt had flowed through the International Development Association, (IDA) and the necessity of replenishing that organization's coffers in the very near future limited further development assistance through this soft aid mechanism. In contemplating the April consortium meeting, Reid wrote to the staff loan committee that even though, strictly speaking, the "scope for further Bank assistance [as opposed to that of other consortium members] was limited by the already high level of India's external debt service,"[20] the Bank might have to ante up a disproportionate amount. Delhi was asking for US$1.25 billion of assistance, and was unlikely to get even US$1 billion from disillusioned providers. (The US$915 million received by the Indians in the first round of pledging eventually became US$1.075 billion after some Bank prodding by consortium members).

As much as it might dislike extending itself further, the Bank could not simply cut off its participation. Moreover, it was anxious to set an example for private banks, which had thus far only financed about US$76 million of the country's development program at competitive rates. Their participation was seen as vital over the longer term and Bank policy was to encourage it at every turn: "In view of the importance the Bank attaches to these sales, would the reaction of the market, and on general grounds of other aid contributors, not be unfavorable if the Bank now stopped its lending to India?" That, of course, was a rhetorical question, and the debt servicing issue would become a much hotter one in the very near future with much Bank time spent figuring out repayment schedules that would not precipitate a collapse in the Indian economy.

From the Bank's perspective, assistance was simply not paying the sort of dividends in terms of the alleviation of poverty that had been hoped for. Since 1958, more money had been loaned than requested, yet "the growth of the economy had fallen far short of Plan expectations, and there [was] no sign that India's dependence on external support [was] being reduced."[21] If there were not encouraging developments soon, the consortium could well fall apart.

The April 1963 pledging session, the first in which Reid participated, sought to address these problems. For the first time, the US representative expressed Washington's opposition to the status quo, and questioned its open-ended commitment to Indian aid, some of which seemed to disappear too quickly into the bank accounts of corrupt civil servants. Other consortium members were also beginning to question openly their allegiance to the program, citing India's rampant corruption and the facts that Indian growth rates had slowed dramatically and per capita income had actually fallen in recent years. The United States, riding point on a group of increasingly uneasy accomplices, argued that the Aid-India consortium needed "a more regular organization which would keep developments in [India] under regular review."[22] The Americans hoped a more "regular organization" might inject some coherence into the process whereby aid money was allocated. This had been debated within the World Bank among officials in SAMED and Reid agreed with the American position. In mid-1963, he noted that it was not possible to "dissent from the view that the [consortium] had not been very effective ... in ensuring that aid to India ... was properly coordinated by the donors and effectively used by the recipients."

The April 1963 meeting also allowed consortium members to talk directly and collectively about India's problems with L.K. Jha, the head of the department of economic affairs in India's ministry of finance. Jha, who was the first senior Indian official to attend these meetings, heard of the consortium's displeasure with the course and pace of Indian development. He also learned of the Bank's growing concern at India's spiralling debt-servicing costs. Woods was blunt and his diagnoses disturbing: "Debt service is already absorbing about one-fifth of India's current receipts on external account, and unless there is a change in the terms of loans and credits, there is every likelihood that this proportion will before long rise above one-quarter."[23] There was not, and it did; eighteen months later the problem had become acute, forcing Jha to meet with Woods in London to discuss debt rescheduling, reduction of interest paid on some of the paper, and the assistance India was to receive.

In Reid's view, India's failure to develop and improve its standard of living could be attributed to its complacency on the agricultural front. Astonishingly, in the decade since 1953, there had been no real increase in agricultural production. Reid had already immersed himself in the problems of Indian agriculture and knew the issues well. Throughout the 1950s, he had presciently written about the benefits of increased agricultural productivity. He passed these thoughts along to Indian ministers and officials whenever the opportunity arose. While still ambassador in Bonn, for instance, he had asked Sir Raghavan Pillai, then one of Nehru's closest advisers, "why [doesn't] India concentrate all its national resources of brain, skill and energy on doubling its agricultural production within ten years. This would give you a firm and safe foundation for industrial development."[24] That was very true.

Reid's interest was evident when he joined the World Bank, and he was determined to press for changes. He thought that the Indian government needed something to "shock" it into a re-evaluation of its agricultural policy. Until this happened, Reid adopted a pessimistic view, expressing "little confidence in the future of India." While the so-called green revolution was just around the corner, the present situation remained perplexing. Financing irrigation projects was, theoretically, one method of increasing production, but loans for those projects had not paid off in the past. As Reid knew, the physical construction of the facilities was but *one* element in ensuring a successful project. It was also the area in which the Bank had invested heavily and with mixed results. Reid, however, was convinced that the IBRD should *not* finance any irrigation project in the country unless it was satisfied that it had done all that it could to ensure that Indian governments, state or federal, provided adequate research and extension services. Moreover, it was not good enough to put "tough, sensible provisions in the project agreements. We must ensure that the undertakings are implemented." It was equally important to ensure proper levels of support for Indian farmers, a field that lay in the jealously guarded jurisdiction of the state government. It was, Reid argued, "the big irrigation projects building for years, with inadequate credit to the farmer to complete the job at the farm level, that stick in the mud."[25]

The Bank was slow to embrace these views. "At the outset," as one historian has noted, "the Bank saw itself more as a capital transfers specialist, less as a comprehensive development promoter obligated to pursue all major aspects of development."[26] Moreover, during the mid-to-late 1950s, modernization theorists argued that industry was the most likely engine of development. Nevertheless, Reid enjoyed some success challenging these ideas. For instance, the loan agreement for the Sone River project was negotiated by SAMED and imposed precise conditions on the northeastern state of Bihar concerning agricultural research and extension work. In exchange for Bank support the state government undertook to conduct research into local living conditions, to provide extension services to rural farmers, and to make agricultural credit available in the region. It was a successful exercise on all sides, and Reid hoped that it could be used as an example for other Indian states.

As long as India's overall economy continued to perform poorly, however, there was little hope that the Bank could use its resources effectively to spur improvements in agricultural productivity. In the months after the April 1963 consortium meeting, the Bank became much more assertive in demanding that New Delhi met certain criteria to eliminate poor planning, inefficiency, and corruption. The Bank wanted an outline plan for Indian development covering the next five years that would include a review of its domestic economic policy. But this soon proved impossible. King reported to Reid, who was responsible for wrestling the plans from India, that no amount of prodding could get the Indians moving. Glumly, he observed, that not even a "Perspective Plan [has emerged] or [been] roughed out."[27] Moreover, he wrote, when Bank officials visited ministers in various state capitals, their "interest was rather unwelcome ... [Krishna] Moorthi [secretary general of the ministry of finance] picked up a word which I had dropped on purpose, namely, that our approach might have been considered 'novel'. I assured him that if it had been novel before, it was novel no longer." The Bank was getting serious with respect to commitments and planning.

It was also looking more seriously on India's failure to take up all the assistance that had been offered by consortium members. This came with a cost to the country and there were numerous instances when New Delhi had not used approved loans that had been requested as a part of its development program. In 1961, for example, India secured a US$35 million loan for the modernization and development of the private coal industry. By July 1964, however, less than US$11 million had been used, with the balance sitting idly in the Bank's vault. As Reid wrote to King, it was one of the "serious consequences of keeping so much aid tied up unproductively – one of the costs of slow project implementation."[28]

The slow pace of project implementation was partly a result of a proliferation of controls "accompanied by laborious procedures."[29] Even "Indian newspapers pointed out [that] 'merely getting the requisite permit and license forms is itself something of an adventure' and access to information and assistance is now only possible through 'touts and intermediaries.'" Moreover, King told Reid, the planning commission was next to useless because of official interference; the commission was "deeply involved in the business of political horse-trading. A recent Bank mission, which was studying methods of assessing irrigation projects, was told by the irrigation adviser that this sort of thing had no point, because everything was decided politically anyway."[30]

Nevertheless, there was soon evidence of movement among some officials and politicians in New Delhi. This was especially true following Nehru's death in May 1964. His successor as prime minister, Lal Bahadur Shastri, was more prepared to contemplate a different approach to development. Shastri also gave ministers such as C.S. Subramaniam, the new minister of agriculture, the powers necessary to undertake reforms. Reid thought him a good choice; he recorded his impressions following a visit to India in October 1964, noting that some "of those who participated in the complicated process of cabinet making ... may have hoped that his appointment to this ministry would finish him politically. But [he] is intelligent, knowledgeable about modern techniques of economic analysis, able to gain the confidence of experts, both Indian and foreign, energetic, and with legitimate grounds for hope that, if he is successful as minister of food and agriculture, he might ... become prime minister of India."[31]

Subramaniam's appointment seemed to suggest that India was now taking agricultural improvement seriously. Reid recorded in his "Impressions of India" memorandum following his October 1964 trip that "whether there exists in India as there ought to a general sense of national humiliation that, seventeen years after independence, Indian agricultural policies have failed to provide sufficient food for the masses at reasonable prices, there does [now] exist a greater willingness by people in authority to face facts."[32] He detected some welcome change in government, among which he included "the downgrading of heavy industry ... in favour of agriculture."

The problems affecting Indian development in general and agriculture in particular had a salubrious effect on government in India, or so the Bank believed. Romano Pantanali, who was appointed the new IBRD resident representative in the capital in July 1964, informed Reid that the country seemed to be in a state of flux. He cited the example of the Indian press, which had adopted a more conciliatory approach to India's relations with the Bank. He suggested that newspapers had gone from writing that "it is none of your business" to "you seem to have a point." The higher cost of rice and wheat had helped focus New Delhi's attention on the rising cost of food. Pantanali was undoubtedly correct in his assessment that "when people shout in the streets, there is no more room for endless and useless arguing."[33] Reid, who observed that "India [was] in an economic morass," could only agree.[34]

The Bank seized upon this deterioration in the Indian situation to push and prod them to reform their civil service, and move toward greater administrative efficiency and sounder economic policies. The regional IBRD staff in India recommended to Reid a more intensive analysis of the country's economic situation than had ever been undertaken before. Reid, in his turn, emphasized this to George Woods, telling him that such an appraisal was a necessary guide to Bank lending policies and to the allocation of IDA resources. It would also be, he noted, a very "delicate task."[35] He suggested a structure for a review committee that would travel to the subcontinent, a suggestion that fell on ready ears. Woods took the advice offered, though he angered both Reid and Bank officials by hiring an outside team headed by the American economist, Bernard Bell, to conduct the survey. It eventually produced a thirteen-volume report in 1965 that comprehensively dissected every aspect of Indian life.

By then, of course, Reid had already left the Bank. There were several reasons for his growing unhappiness in Washington. First, he often found the Bank's conservative ideology and operational code frustrating. His efforts to support agricultural development, though successful, were wearing. He was also tired of the Bank's slow pace and overarching bureaucracy. When he tried to commit US$100 million of Bank money and US$140 million of IDA money into projects over eight months instead of a year, he was criticized for moving too fast. In Reid's view, he was there for two reasons: to "assist India in its efforts to speed up the pace of its economic development [... and ...] also put pressure on the Bank to speed up the pace of its activities ... and I think this kind of pressure on our colleagues at the Bank is necessary. I have a strong feeling that there is danger of a certain flabbiness in some of the departments of the Bank which results from their working too seldom under the pressure of deadlines."[36]

Finally, and perhaps most important, Reid was never comfortable with his relationship with the Bank's president, George Woods. Indeed, with the passing of time, Reid soon found himself frequently bypassed in the chain of command even on important matters for which he was responsible. For example, in circulating his impressions of a conversation he had had with L.K. Jha on the subject of the ways and means of making progress in rescheduling the early maturities of India's external debt,

Woods ignored Reid and his interest in this topic. Indeed, this had been one of the files on which the director had been concentrating and his omission from the circulation list appended to the memorandum was striking and unexpected.[37]

Even as early as April 1963, with the federal election victory of Prime Minister Lester B. Pearson and his Liberal Party, Reid would have returned to Ottawa had a position been offered. In the fall of that year he went so far as to enquire what the possibilities might be, writing to Pearson that he would be "happy to return to Ottawa and join his team."[38] The circumstances were unpromising. In January 1964, he expressed interest in the position of director general of the External Aid Office then being established in Ottawa.[39] In September 1964, Murray Ross, president of the newly-established York University, asked him if he would become the first principal of Glendon College. He deferred his decision until mid-November, in the interim writing again to Pearson, noting that "you know how happy I would be to work in Ottawa on your team in a position where I would be able to use my abilities in the service of my ccuntry."[40] The prime minister urged him to take up Ross's offer, which he did.

Though he remained on the Bank's roster until June 1965, Reid was effectively gone by New Year's Day 1965. Those six months were taken up researching and writing a monograph entitled *The Future of the World Bank*. It was a searching and insightful critique of the IBRD's past practices and future prospects that stressed the need for the World Bank to tailor its lending to local conditions in the developing world. Though the report was well received in the international banking community, (and many of the issues raised by Reid were eventually addressed by the Bank), it was not much of a professional legacy. Nor had Reid's time in Washington been personally satisfying. As he noted in his valedictory address, the name of his department had been recently changed from SAMED to South Asia Department, or SAD. And this was, he thought, entirely appropriate. He was content to return home after twelve years abroad, even if he was not to receive a coveted appointment in the Department of External Affairs. Glendon beckoned, and he would respond to the call, tougher and wiser, having been exposed to the difficulties of international banking. He would need all that experience, and more, at Glendon.

NOTES

1 Escott Reid to Norman Smith, 13 February 1962, Reid Papers, Volume 36, file: Smith, I. Norman, 2 of 3 (6), 1947–1984, National Archives of Canada (NAC).

2 Douglas Small, Escott Reid Colloquium, Glendon College, 5 October 2001.

3 See Escott Reid to Norman Smith, 10 November 1960, Reid Papers, Volume 36, file: Smith, I Norman, 2 of 3 (6), 1947–1984, NAC.

4 Escott Reid, *Radical Mandarin* (Toronto: University of Toronto Press, 1989), 324.

5 Devesh Kapur, John P. Lewis, and Richard Webb, *The World Bank: Its First Half Century, Volume 1: History* (Washington, D.C.: Brookings Institute Press, 1997), 14.

6 Reid, *Radical Mandarin*, 338.

7 Escott Reid, "Impressions of Some of the Issues Before the Bank and IDA," 2 October 1962, Reid Papers, Volume 37, file: International Bank for Reconstruction and Development, NAC.

8 Kapur, Lewis, and Webb, *The World Bank*, 143. See also Jagdish Bhagwati, *India in Transition: Freeing the Economy* (Oxford: Oxford University Press, 1993), 8.

9 Escott Reid to Ben King, 21 October 1963, World Bank Records, Box 57, Central Files 1946–1971, Operational Correspondence – India, World Bank Archives (WBA).

10 Escott Reid, "Some Impressions of India," 19 March 1963, Reid Papers, Volume 37, file: International Bank for Reconstruction and Development Operational Memoranda, 1962–1964, 1 of 2, NAC.

11 Escott Reid to Ben King, 7 October 1965, World Bank Records, Box 57, Central Files 1946–1971, Operational Correspondence – India, WBA.

12 Ben King to Donald Jeffries, 25 April 1963, World Bank Records, Box 52, file: India – Consortium Meeting – April–May 1963, Central Files, 1946–1971, Operational Correspondence – India, WBA.

13 Escott Reid to Burke Knapp, 30 January 1963, World Bank Records, Box 53, file: India – Consortium Meeting, 8 February 1963, Central Files, 1946–1971, Operational Correspondence – India, WBA.

14 Ben King to Escott Reid, 24 October 1963, World Bank Records, Box 54, file: India – Aid Consortium 1962–1965, India Consortium Meeting Feb–Mar 64, WBA.

15 Ben King to Escott Reid, 3 October 1963, World Bank Records, Box 52, Central Files 1946–1971, Operational Correspondence – India, WBA.

16 Escott Reid to Ben King, 20 November 1963, World Bank Records, Box 54, Central files 1946–1971, Operational Correspondence – India, WBA.

17 Bhagwati, *India in Transition*, 10. Similarly, as Kapur, Lewis, and Webb point out, in the 1950s "all the Western world thought India did everything right ... but suddenly in the 1960s, everybody felt that it was all going sour." See *The World Bank*, 214.

18 "Minutes of Seventh Meeting on India's Foreign Exchange Situation – 30 April and 1 May 1963." World Bank Records, Box 52, Central files 1946–1971, Operational Correspondence – India, WBA.

19 Peter Wright to Escott Reid, 11 June 1963, World Bank Records, Box 53, Central Files 1946–1971, Operational Correspondence – India, WBA.

20 Escott Reid, Memorandum from Department of Operations, South Asia and Middle East, "India – Bank/IDA Assistance for Third Year of Third Plan," 11 April 1963, World Bank Records, Box 53, file: India – Consortium Meeting June–August 1963, Central Files, 1946–1971, Operational Correspondence – India, WBA.

21 George Woods to Desai, 20 June 1963, World Bank Records, Box 41, Central Files 1946–1971, Operational Correspondence – India, WBA.

22 Ben King to Alexander Stevenson, 8 February 1963, World Bank Records, Box 52, file: India – Consortium Meeting June–August 1963, Central Files, 1946– 1971, Operational Correspondence – India, WBA. Between 1949 and March 1966, the total assistance extended to India by the Bank was approximately US$1.85 billion, with US$1.2 billion going as regular loans and the rest from the IDA. See Briefing Notes for Meeting with Indian Delegation, 8 September 1964, World Bank Records, Box 71, file: Central Files 1946–1971, Operational Correspondence India – WBA.

23 George Woods, "Seventh Meeting on India's Foreign Exchange Situation," 30 April 1963, World Bank Records, Box 71, file: Central Files 1946–1971, Operational Correspondence India – WBA.

24 Escott Reid to Ben King, 20 November 1963, World Bank Records, Box 53, Central Files 1946–1971, Operational Correspondence – India, WBA.

25 Ben King to Alexander Stevenson, 17 October 1963. World Bank Records, Box 53, Central Files 1946–1971, Operational Correspondence – India, WBA.

26 Kapur, Lewis, and Webb, *The World Bank*, 381.

27 Ben King to Escott Reid, 13 September 1963, World Bank Records, Box 52, Central Files 1946–1971, Operational Correspondence – India, WBA.

28 Escott Reid to Ben King, 16 January 1964, World Bank Records, Box 69, Central Files 1946–1971, Operational Correspondence – India, WBA.

29 Ben King to Escott Reid, "Draft Brief," 27 April 1964, World Bank Records, Box 70, Central Files 1946–1971, Operational Correspondence – India, WBA.

30 Escott Reid to Tarlok Singh, 19 June 1963, World Bank Records, Box 52, Central Files 1946–1971, Operational Correspondence – India, WBA.

31 Escott Reid, "Impressions of India: October 1964," 26 October 1964, World Bank Records, Box 71, Central Files 1946–1971, Operational Correspondence – India, WBA.

32 Ibid.

33 Romano Pantanali to Escott Reid, 25 August 1964, World Bank Records, Box 70, Central Files 1946–1971, Operational Correspondence – India, WBA.

34 Escott Reid, "Impressions of India: October 1964," 26 October 1964, World Bank Records, Box 71, Central Files 1946–1971, Operational Correspondence – India, WBA.

35 Escott Reid to George Woods, 8 May 1964, World Bank Records, Box 69, Central Files 1946–1971, Operational Correspondence – India, WBA.

36 Escott Reid to Ben King, 16 October 1963, World Bank Records, Box 69, Central Files 1946–1971, Operational Correspondence – India, WBA. See also Reid, *Radical Mandarin*, 325.

37 George Woods to file, "India – Visit with Mr. L.K. Jha in London, November 8, 1964," 22 November 1964, World Bank Records, Box 76, Central Files 1946–1971, Operational Correspondence – India, WBA.

38 Escott Reid to L.B. Pearson, 23 September 1963, Escott Reid Papers, Volume 29, file: Pearson, L.B. (6) 1948–1973, NAC.

39 Escott Reid to A.E. Ritchie, 6 January 1964, Escott Reid Papers, Volume 35, NAC.

40 Escott Reid to L.B. Pearson, September 1964, Escott Reid Papers, Volume 29, file: Pearson, L.B. (6) 1948–1973, NAC.

6 The Glendon College Experiment

ALYSON KING

"Mine is the opportunity, this afternoon, to express my faith in you, my belief in your capacity to wear conscience and involvement as a mantle of honour; my belief also that your generation of restless social activists will find the resources of mind and heart to translate your hopes into positive lasting achievement wherever there is a human need – and that is everywhere."

Prime Minister Lester B. Pearson to the students of Glendon College,
30 September 1966

Escott Reid arrived at York University's Glendon College in early January 1965. He was charged with creating a unique and intimate place of learning that would be fully bilingual, fully residential, and offer a small but demanding curriculum: a liberal arts college in the Oxford tradition. But this proved a difficult and challenging assignment. Reid appeared on Glendon's wooded campus just as the university system in Canada headed off in dramatically new directions. Pressured by governments to meet the post-secondary educational needs of the sprawling generation of post-war baby-boomers, old universities expanded and new ones shot up overnight. In the scramble for funding and resources that accompanied this expansion of Ontario's network of universities, Reid's initial vision for Glendon College was quickly challenged by university administrators and faculty as costly and impractical. Reid fought back and soon cemented his reputation as hard to work with and tough to manage. The difficulties Reid confronted at Glendon were exacerbated by the new generation of students that appeared on campus in the mid-1960s. Affluent consumers of sex, drugs, and rock 'n' roll, they rejected the established patterns of student life and strongly opposed the structures of university governance. They too would severely test Reid's diplomatic skills.

"The Plum of Canadian Universities": Confronting the Administration

Glendon College was, and still is, a college of York University. Founded on 26 March 1959, York University was intended to address a lack of space in Ontario's universities for qualified high school students and to ease overcrowding at the University of Toronto. For the first academic year, 1960–61, York held courses in Falconer Hall on University Avenue but it was soon clear that a larger space would be needed. As a result, the University of Toronto offered up the Glendon campus, formerly the Wood estate and home to the university's law school.

In the original conception of York, the entire university was to be housed at Glendon and initial plans for a university that would accommodate about 3,500 students were drawn up by Thomas Howarth, the director of the school of architecture at the University of Toronto. When it became apparent that York would have to take on many more students, the first president, Murray Ross, launched a new plan for the university. His design included a large multi-faculty university for both commuting and residential students (York campus), an evening college for part-time degree students (Atkinson College), and a small residential college (Glendon College).

The idea for a small, liberal arts college was part of Ross's overall vision for York University as early as October 1960. When the search for the first principal got underway in late 1964, it was already clear that the college was to have an emphasis on public affairs. By early 1965, Ross and the Council of the Faculty of Arts and Science had decided that Glendon would offer honours programs in economics, political science, sociology, history, English, French, and philosophy – all subjects that included a heavy dose of civic virtue.[1] Ross thought that Escott Reid, an experienced diplomat and influential civil servant, might be ideally suited for the new college with its commitment to public service. Although Reid had no experience in university administration and had

taught only one session at Dalhousie University in the late 1930s, his academic credentials were solid. He was an honours graduate of the University of Toronto and had attended Oxford University as a Rhodes Scholar.
On his return to Canada in 1930, he won an award from the Rockefeller
Foundation to conduct doctoral research on Canadian political parties,
and produced a highly respected series of articles. The rapid growth of
new universities in the early 1960s most certainly made highly-qualified
candidates scarce. Indeed, Reid was not the only civil servant appointed
as principal of a university college in the mid-1960s. His former colleagues, Douglas LePan and Wynne Plumptre, were recruited to
Toronto's University College (1964) and Scarborough College (1965)
respectively. Both LePan and Plumptre had been lured from promising
academic careers to the civil service during the Second World War.[2] In
the summer of 1964, Ross offered Reid the position of Principal of Glendon College for a five-year term.

   Although frustrated with his current job with the World Bank and anxious to return to Canada, Reid was not enthusiastic about the prospect of
working at Glendon. He consulted with his family and with a number of
close friends in universities across Canada before accepting Ross's offer.
After the suffocating bureaucracy of the World Bank, aspects of the position were clearly attractive, and Escott reported to his son, Timothy, that
"there would be a great deal of autonomy in the job, that the board of
governors is a first rate one, that there is a determination to create a liberal arts college of high quality, and that it could be one of the most fascinating jobs in Canadian life."[3] His son, who was employed as Ross's
assistant, concurred, arguing the "Principalship of Glendon College is
one of, if not 'the' plum in Canadian universities. You'll have to see it to
appreciate it."[4] Others, though more guarded in their advice, were also
encouraging. Norman MacKenzie, a former president of the University
of British Columbia and a member of the Senate of Canada, advised
Reid that if "the set up satisfies you in the terms you and Murray Ross
describe, I would urge you to take it. It should be a good show and great
fun. Murray is an old and good friend of mine, and I foresee no trouble
with him – save that he may not be able to deliver all he would like or
has promised."[5]

   But Reid still wanted to return to the centre of action in Ottawa. Since
late 1963, he had been actively discussing the possibility of taking over
Canada's new External Aid Office with Prime Minister L.B. Pearson and
Paul Martin, the secretary of state for external affairs. Martin, however,

rejected Reid's demand that the overseas aid office report directly to the minister, insisting that the agency report to the under-secretary of state for external affairs, Marcel Cadieux. With his typical arrogance, Reid told Martin that "I don't intend to serve under [Cadieux]. He was my junior for twenty years." Unable to resolve the impasse, Pearson suggested that Reid accept the Glendon offer.[6] Reid continued to delay. In September he wrote Pearson, repeating his wish to join "your team in a position where I would be able to use my abilities in the service of my country." The prime minister was not forthcoming, and urged Reid to take up the job at Glendon.[7]

Reluctantly, Reid was persuaded, and in January 1965 he agreed to serve as Glendon's first principal on the understanding that the university was committed to the project in terms of finances and resources. For Reid, the actions of both Ross and York's board of governors over the next four years raised serious doubts about that commitment.

Evidence that Ross had promised more than he could deliver emerged soon enough. The protracted negotiations over Reid's terms of employment hinted that there was trouble to come and foreshadowed his lengthy power struggles with the president and York's board of governors for control over Glendon. Reid took considerable care thinking about the implications of the job and his prospects for success, in part because he took a cut in salary and pension benefits in accepting it. In compensation, he insisted that the university provide on-campus housing with meals and housekeeping service included, and an expense account for entertaining as principal. Reid's insistence on adequate housing for himself and his wife also reflected the importance that Reid placed on Glendon being a fully residential college; it was important that he, too, live on campus. While his notes and the formal offer from Ross show that details about his housing had been agreed upon, the appointment approved by the board of governors included only an unfurnished apartment.[8] In the end, after considerable bickering, the university and Reid compromised: Glendon would provide kitchen equipment, curtains, and furniture for the "public rooms" while the Reids furnished their sitting room and bedroom themselves.[9] It was not an auspicious beginning.

Once on board, Reid turned his attention to fleshing out the details of the philosophy and curriculum of the new college and to ensuring that the physical requirements for the college were in the works. He was strongly influenced by his memories of both the University of Toronto and Oxford University in the 1920s and 1930s. Indeed, his old friend, the

Carleton University historian Frank Underhill, warned Reid that "I think you tend to idealize a little too much the old Oxford college."[10] The Oxford influence was even evident in his plans for the designs of the women's and men's residences. In a letter to Ross, Reid noted that the men's residences should have "vertical houses," while the women's should be horizontal.[11] The differences in design reflected both the Oxford influence – the original men's residences at Oxford were built in a style sometimes referred to as "staircase" or "vertical" – and different attitudes towards men versus women students. The vertical style affords more privacy and less opportunity for surveillance by those in charge, so the men students had more freedom to come and go as they pleased. The horizontal style planned for women students allowed for easier surveillance of the students and therefore less freedom of movement. These differences, as well as discrepancies in the rules of conduct for men and women, would not pass unnoticed by a generation of women committed to notions of gender equality, who would eventually fight Reid to have the regulations revised.

When Reid turned his attention to finalizing plans for the college, he continued to solicit the advice of others. Frank Underhill, for example, told him early in 1965 that the curriculum plans for Glendon were lacking. He felt that science should be included "as a completely equal partner with the humanities" and that without sociology in the mix, "[m]odern history and political science remained stranded in the nineteenth century."[12] Glendon, Underhill believed, was going to be at a disadvantage because of its geographical separation from the rest of York University. The research library and laboratories would be located on the main campus and Glendon students and faculty would also miss out on the stimulation of contacts with other students and faculty members from outside the college. In order for Glendon to be the exhilarating environment that Reid envisioned, staff would have to be "much more devoted to teaching in all its informal aspects and in its contacts with students than any contemporary staff in North America is likely to be."[13] Underhill also believed that Canadian students were not sufficiently mature to do well without the guidance of graduate students:

You intend, I take it, to make it an undergraduate college. But our Canadian undergraduates are very immature intellectually. They are not on the level of the students in an Oxford college who have been reading much more adult literature than our students have. You ought to consider a leaven of graduate students mixed in with them. They will help to encourage intellectual influences inside the college community and to dilute the interest in sport and 'student self-government' (this last activity seems to use up a portentous amount of the energies of the more voluble undergraduates at Carleton).[14]

While Underhill considered Glendon College an excellent idea, he clearly thought that Reid had hard work ahead. Norman MacKenzie also feared that Reid faced a real challenge. MacKenzie felt that Reid's plan to recruit French Canadians as both faculty and students was good, but that it would be difficult to implement, as it certainly turned out to be. MacKenzie also warned Reid that some members of the board of governors were unsure whether Reid's plans could be implemented as quickly as he would like. He advised Reid to "recognize the difficulties and the problems of a new institution, and while setting for yourselves and for all concerned the programme that you want and expect and intend to carry out, you should be prepared to cooperate with your colleagues in any solution of their problems and be patient if all of your own desires are not fulfilled as soon as you would like."[15] MacKenzie's apprehensions reflected his own considerable experience with universities in Canada and indeed proved accurate.

It was apparent almost as soon as Reid began to take charge of Glendon's operations that he was going to face more opposition than he had anticipated from the board of governors over his initial plans. Edgar McInnis, chairman of the Glendon College planning committee and dean of York's Faculty of Graduate Studies, warned Reid in March 1965, that it was "clear in the discussions of the committee that not all the initial proposals of the Principal-Designate can count on unanimous or even majority support."[16] Reid faced further difficulties in getting Senate support for his various initiatives. A statement issued by the Senate in June 1965 outlining its understanding of Glendon's bilingual mission, for example, clearly did not accord with Reid's. Where Reid, who was himself unilingual, saw bilingualism as essential to Glendon's future, York's Senators viewed it simply "with sympathy."[17] Ross tried to be optimistic, telling Reid "that many members of the Senate supported the statement less because of a conviction about the validity of the idea, than a desire to help you develop a programme about which you feel strongly. I think it is a quite generous statement and provides you with the opportunity to do what you wished."[18] But this was not enough. In an exchange of letters with Ross, Reid insisted on written confirmation that the Senate fully supported his plans. Without it, he felt he could not proceed with hiring department heads. By that September, Reid had his statement.[19]

Reid was uncomfortable working within the university's small and petty bureaucracy. His natural enthusiasm for simply getting things done bogged down in the slow process of submitting even the most basic questions and recommendations to Ross, who then took them to the board of governors. The process left Reid frustrated and disheartened. Indeed, he commented in his memoirs that "the red tape of universities was worse than the red tape of governments."[20] Moreover, as a senior public servant in Ottawa during the 1940s and 1950s, Reid had been able to operate independently and quietly, through an established "old boys" network. Not surprisingly, such an operating style soon got Reid into trouble at Glendon. By the middle of July 1965, he had discreetly approached several candidates for department headships at the college, making what he considered to be firm offers. He fully expected that his candidates, because of their experience and stature, would not have to be approved by John T. Saywell, the Dean of Arts and Science. In his early thirties, Saywell was considerably younger than Reid, who must have found it galling that such a "young pup" had veto power over his staffing decisions.[21] In a letter to Ross, Reid argued that "I have reservations about the applicability to Glendon College of the procedures set forth in Dean Saywell's letter not only about these five people [to whom he had made offers] but other possible appointments as chairmen. It would certainly be my hope that I would not offer the chairmanship of any department to someone who would require many letters of reference."[22] Not surprisingly, in a matter of such importance, the university initially refused to budge, and Reid submitted his candidates to Saywell for approval. Over time, Reid gradually wore down Ross's and Saywell's resistance and Reid's determination to hire the people he wanted prevailed in the end.[23]

Frustrated by these kinds of procedural delays, Reid was not inclined to compromise. He tolerated little opposition and reacted strongly to any challenge to his vision of Glendon. On at least four occasions he even threatened to resign in order to get his way. He issued his first threat during the summer of 1965 during the battle to secure formal Senate support for his view of Glendon as a bilingual college. He told his old friend John Holmes that he would step down from the principalship if his problems could not be overcome.[24] In early September 1965, only three months after formally starting the job, he again considered resigning. In a memorandum to Ross, Reid complained that he had only just learned about a recommendation by the building committee that the building of a second residence be deferred. He strongly opposed this proposal, contending that if the college did not become fully residential as soon as possible, he would have to recommend postponing its opening. He pointedly asked how so important a decision was made without his input and demanded an explanation, declaring that "I would not find it possible to continue as Principal of Glendon College if I am not given adequate opportunities to participate in the process of making decisions affecting Glendon College."[25]

The continued uncertainty surrounding Glendon College's financing also raised Reid's frequent ire, and prompted additional threats to leave Glendon. In the early part of 1966, for example, Reid wrote to Ross with details regarding his proposed budget. He emphasized that Glendon had unique expenses compared with other York colleges and stressed his long administrative experience in setting up and running offices. He concluded the letter by insisting that "[m]y position on the question of my continued association with York University remains as it was when I sent you my draft letter of February 14th. I do not consider that it would be appropriate for me to remain as Principal of Glendon College if I were to consider that the funds provided by the Board of Governors for Glendon College for the year 1966–67 were not sufficient to enable it to move at a reasonable speed in that year towards its publicly declared objectives."[26] Clearly Reid felt that he had put his own reputation behind the project but if the university was not willing to support it adequately, he wanted no part of it.

Despite Reid's threats to resign, Glendon's financial situation improved only slightly, and budgetary questions again brought Reid into conflict with York's board of governors. In 1967, Glendon's continuing financial difficulties and the low enrollment figures anticipated for the upcoming academic year were so serious that Ross told Reid that he doubted whether Glendon could support seven honours programs and ensure their quality. He suggested that Glendon offer only three, "but certainly not more than five, subjects."[27] A year later, in May 1968, Reid wrote a long letter to Ross outlining Glendon's need for special financial consideration for the upcoming year. Without the academic appointments that Dean H.S. Harris had recommended, Reid argued that "it will not be possible for

Glendon College to operate and ... both the University and the College will be seriously embarrassed if the pending appointments are not confirmed at the earliest possible moment."[28] Reid thought that one possible solution might be to use his extensive political contacts to seek other sources of revenue from governments, foundations, corporations, and private citizens. That Reid, who had made it clear on his appointment that he planned to leave fund-raising to the university, was even considering a fund-raising campaign illustrated the extent of Glendon's crisis.

During the fall of 1968, Reid approached various government offices for advice on how to attain special funding for Glendon's unique programme. He sent letters, brochures, and other documents to John P. Robarts, premier of Ontario, Pierre Trudeau, the prime minister of Canada, and J.J. Carson, chairman of the Public Service Commission of Canada. He hoped that the enactment of the federal government's official languages act would help generate support for Glendon's bilingual programme.[29] Reid reported the results of his preliminary contacts to Ross in December, noting optimistically that various government officials were supportive of Glendon College.[30] In the spring of 1969, without consulting Ross, Reid drafted an "Appeal for Financial Support for Glendon College."[31] But Reid was very quickly blocked by York's board of governors, which felt he was overstepping his bounds with the appeal. The board also resented Reid's tactics, and thought he was putting excessive pressure on them through some of his publicity measures.[32]

During the last half of Reid's tenure at Glendon, fears about Glendon's survival persisted, largely as a result of, as Michiel Horn has described it, a "paranoia"[33] that the board of governors wanted to shut the college down. This sense of paranoia is not surprising given the struggles Reid faced over financing, curriculum, recruitment and retention of students and faculty, and the student protests, which seemed to be escalating. This feeling was also fueled by complaints that the main York campus was subsidizing the Glendon experiment to its own detriment.[34] When Murray Ross proposed establishing a presidential committee on Glendon College, known as the Gardiner Committee, Reid and the Glendon faculty understood that the committee's focus would be on the "development and strengthening" of the college. Within two weeks of the proposal, Reid asked Ross to address the "rumours which [had] spread about the reasons and nature of the proposed presidential committee on Glendon College."[35] There was a strong fear that Glendon's higher expenses would reflect badly on the College in the eyes of the Gardiner Committee. Then in March 1969 a rumour spread that Glendon was to become an institute of public administration, "a sort of staff college for civil servants," that would be run by the government.[36] Both Reid and Dean Harris believed that this rumour might be true, and they feared that Ross was not providing an adequate response to their questions. Ross, however, felt that Reid was overreacting: "I cannot believe you wish deliberately to distort our discussions or to create a crisis where one does not exist, but it would be difficult to escape this conclusion."[37] On 10 March the board of governors assured Reid that it had no plans to close Glendon, nor had it taken part in any discussions of this type.[38]

"He had style and a lot of courage": Reid and His Faculty

Reid's tenure at Glendon was also strained, although to a lesser degree, by faculty challenges to the operation of the college and its curriculum. The biggest controversy arose over the issue of compulsory English classes for all students, anglophone and francophone alike. The concept of compulsory French and English language instruction was a key part of the Glendon curriculum from the start. One colleague wrote to Reid that the "most revolutionary, and the most outstandingly original and valuable idea, to me, is the establishment of the English language as the core of the whole scheme of learning." He went on to say "nearly all Canadian students are fundamentally handicapped by ignorance of the language. They have no respect for it, they are not curious about it."[39] He warned, however, that it was going to be difficult to implement, partially because the instructors themselves would not be well enough prepared to judge the quality of English used in essays or to write it well themselves.

In the fall of 1968 compulsory English came under attack by Michael Gregory, chairman of the English department. At a meeting of the curriculum committee on 15 October 1968, the committee decided to recommend to the faculty council that English should no longer be compulsory. Reid was outraged. He felt betrayed by Gregory, who had brought forward the recommendation despite informing Reid that he did not intend to do so at this meeting. Because Reid understood that the issue was not going to be raised, he did not attend the meeting. More important, Reid explained, the Senate had approved the core concept of Glendon College as "insistence upon skill in the use and appreciation of the English language."[40] When Reid had invited Gregory to join Glendon's English department, the principal had made it clear that an English course would be required in both first and second years and that the emphasis would be on language rather than literature. Reid claimed that Gregory had not only supported this concept, but also found it "very attractive and stimulating."

Reid then outlined other concerns. The assumption underlying the English requirement was that "clarity of language and clarity of thought go together."[41] Eliminating compulsory English, Reid cautioned, would also have financial implications and could negatively affect recruitment of both faculty and students. Moreover, two years was not enough time to realize fully the benefits of such an experiment. Reid suggested that the college move to one compulsory English course rather than two, which would still help students to master the language. The faculty council, however, agreed with Gregory and voted to abolish compulsory English for both first and second year students and also decided to consider eliminating other required courses.[42] This did not sit well with Reid. In another memo to Dean Harris, Reid wrote: "I will *not* support in the Senate the dropping of English. Let Gregory do it."[43] In the end, Reid and the faculty council compromised; English remained compulsory for francophone students and French compulsory for anglophone students for the first two years of their university education. Significantly, Reid's efforts ensured that Glendon retained its defining bilingual flavour.

"Is he the guy with the dog?": Dealing with the Students

Reid's relationship with the students was perhaps more interesting, challenging, and rewarding than his struggles with the administration and the faculty. The students whom Reid confronted when he arrived at Glendon in the mid-1960s were not an easy group to handle. The 1960s was a time of campus unrest and rebellion, and Glendon students were certainly not immune from the influences of the student movement abroad. In the United States students successfully demanded free speech on campus, fought for greater civil rights in the South, and took to the streets to protest the bloody war in Vietnam. Glendon students also had local examples to follow. In 1967 the controversial community school, Rochdale College, was established in downtown Toronto. Within two years students at Montreal's Sir George Williams University were facing down both university administrators and the police in a riot that destroyed the university's computer facilities and left an ugly memory. The causes of the different movements were varied, but all served to make Glendon's students more radical.[44]

Reid's relationship with this radicalized student body did not get off to a good start. When he first moved into his residence in Glendon Hall, he offended students by neglecting to "introduce himself" and by erecting chains across the driveway without consulting or informing the students. The incident was widely reported in the student newspaper *Pro Tem* as well as the *Toronto Star* and the *Globe and Mail*. Many of the students who were interviewed did not know who Reid was, and one asked: "Escott Reid. Is he the guy with dog?"[45] Reid eventually corrected this "diplomatic error" by hosting a holiday dinner for students in his home.[46]

But worse was still to come. During the 1965–66 academic year, Reid was already in residence in Glendon while established York students completed their programs on the Glendon campus. In January 1966 the new principal gave his first formal talk at the college to these transitional students. In it, he outlined his plans for a liberal arts, residence-based university that offered a "revolutionary curriculum" with compulsory English and French courses. Moreover, Reid promised, the new university would offer a rich and varied social life to its students.[47] Modelled on the Oxford tradition, Reid held forth the prospect of dressing for dinner and having a formal high table for faculty members.

Reaction to Reid's plans for Glendon among politicians, students, and the media was hostile. Kenneth Bryden, a member of the provincial legislature for the left-wing New Democratic Party, called it a school for snobs. "The students there are going to be prepared for a life of feeding at the public trough at the expense of working people all over the world. Why else teach them dining protocol. State dinners are going to be the order of the day for them because they are going to be at the top of the heap."[48] Student critics at Glendon were just as harsh. In *Pro Tem* Garth Jowett charged that Glendon would not even be a real university, merely a subsidiary college of York University. Moreover, Glendon would not be universally accessible at a time when the trend at universities was for increased accessibility. Jowett pointed out that the lack of a married student residence, when residence was to be an admission requirement, effectively excluded "a large and vital force" from Glendon. He dismissed the French language requirement as little more than a token attempt to make York "international in flavour" and attacked the compulsory nature of the new curriculum. "[T]he courses in French and English [would] be a challenge, but they represent all that is inherently bad in our Grade Thirteen System [sic]. The province has finally learned that the Grade thirteen curriculum of compulsory subjects is not acceptable to those who by dint of their mentality or stubbornness wish for a little mental stimulation."[49]

In contrast to his stubbornness in dealing with Ross and the board of governors, Reid showed considerable sympathy and flexibility in dealing with students and their increasing activism and criticism. Undoubtedly this was related to his own period of youthful rebellion and social activism, which he had long suspected was being reflected in the social unrest of the 1960s. "My impression is that the generation of the sixties may be as politically-minded as the generation of the thirties," he wrote to his friend Norman Smith, the associate editor of the *Ottawa Journal*. "This encourages me since our world is not likely to survive in peace and freedom unless our best brains go into politics."[50] As a result, Reid was inclined to listen to student views and take them seriously. He particularly delighted in intellectual engagements with students and readily learned from them. Student leaders, as one of their number, Rick Schultz, later recalled, came to respect and trust Reid in spite of his patrician air. Although Reid came to Glendon with little experience in dealing with students, he soon gained the respect of the student body because he was always willing to engage in debate and never talked down to them. Schultz and other student leaders knew that Reid would listen to their arguments and, once convinced, would stand by the students even against the York administration.[51] Indeed, even when Prime Minister Lester B. Pearson formally opened Glendon, Reid allowed students to protest and demand more financial aid.[52] Reid's recognition that the students had the right to voice their opinions was further demonstrated when he handed Pearson and Ontario education minister William Davis a petition signed by 550 faculty members and students protesting the withdrawal of scholarships promised to students in the previous two federal elections and the inadequacies of the Ontario Student Award Program.[53]

Reid made clear his views on student radicals in a speech, entitled "Responsibility and Revolt in Universities," that he gave to Glendon's student body in late September 1967. In it he declared that "I shall be disappointed if Glendon College does not have a higher proportion of restless social activists than most other colleges in Canada."[54] He thought that the college's orientation toward public affairs should encourage social activism, and he believed that the college needed students who questioned and rebelled against the established social order to produce a fruitful kind of intellectual ferment. He assured his audience that there would always be a place for such students at Glendon, and underlined his willingness to work with them through student representatives on Glendon's various governing committees. "[T]here will not, as long as I am Principal," Reid told the assembly, "be an explosion because students have not been adequately consulted on matters which, in my opinion, are of direct concern to them."

He cautioned, however, that student representation created both opportunities and problems for students and faculty. The right to consultation did not, he insisted, imply the right to a veto. Moreover, he added, consultation and collaboration would not "eliminate all the tension at Glendon College."[55] Students and their representatives must use their power in the university in a responsible fashion. Increasingly, he feared that his students were becoming "obsessed with the moral problems of the use and abuse of power" and failing to put what power they did have to good use.[56]

Reid's convictions were soon put to the test. Early in the 1968–69 academic year Glendon's student council launched its "Liber-Action" campaign. This significant challenge to the college's authority was intended to create an environment at Glendon that was "truly alive" by instigating "extensive academic experimentation." The student council advocated the idea that "every member of the College should be able to pursue his [sic] education in whatever manner is deemed best by him. This denies compulsory courses, evaluative processes, and any rule or regulation not agreed to by members of the College as individuals and as a group."[57] There were two aspects to the campaign. First, the students wanted to see the creation of "people-generated courses." Students who wanted to learn about particular topics would come together spontaneously in self-directed study groups. They could approach a faculty member to serve as a resource person, but there would be no credits, examinations, or grades. Second, students would not register in formal courses until after they had had a chance to sample a number of classes. Some students, it was felt, might decide to pay their fees, but not register in any courses in order to educate themselves within the university community.[58] The student council argued that this format would be intellectually stimulating and would prove that Glendon was "not bound by rigid regulations but [was] willing to allow fundamental academic experimentation."[59]

The student council also produced a manifesto entitled "A University is for the People." The manifesto aimed to provoke discussion and controversy, to provide a solid theoretical base for the actions of the student council in the upcoming year, and to inform members of the student union of the position of its elected representatives. While the general goals of Glendon College remained worthy, the student council argued that the college's capacity to achieve its objectives was hampered by "the same factors which are weakening the value of the contemporary university to society. We find at Glendon the same process of evaluation, the same rigidities of administration and social stratification that are choking the university."[60]

The student council called for six specific remedies. Some, such as the demand that the college hire bilingual faculty in all subject areas, were ones that Reid had been struggling to meet from the start. Others were more radical. The students wanted to abolish the faculty, student, and residence councils and amalgamate the three bodies into one elected college government that would be chosen democratically by all members of the Glendon community. They also wanted to do away with all "evaluative processes," and dismantle "formal course structures, compulsory and non-compulsory."[61]

Reid and Glendon could hardly meet all these demands. As Dean Harris pointed out in a memorandum to faculty, 400 students trying to shop around for courses would result in a "chaotic struggle to get seats." More important, the Glendon administration worried that the provincial government might consider "people-generated courses" as extracurricular and reduce the College's operating grant accordingly.[62] However, Reid did implement those changes he thought were feasible, even if they went against his sense of propriety. For example, he quickly met the student council's demand that the college remove "all symbols which contribute to the social stratification of various members or groups of the Glendon community."[63] Even though he felt it would be undignified for older women faculty members to share washrooms with women students, the separate faculty facilities were opened to all members of the college.

Similarly, the head table with service was eliminated and faculty members lined up in the cafeteria alongside the students.[64]

Reid also took the manifesto to the faculty council where its more far-reaching proposals were turned over to various committees, which in turn asked the student council to submit briefs to them on each proposal. The faculty committees also asked the student council to consider some specific questions about the proposals and made the point that they were willing to look sympathetically at them.[65] By turning to the students, Reid was effectively pushing them to accept responsibility for coming up with realistic solutions to the problems that they saw in the college. It was a successful strategy, and by late September *Excalibur*, the York student newspaper, reported that almost all new and returning students had enrolled in their classes.[66] By the time Reid left Glendon at the end of 1969, students were members of almost all college committees. When his son and daughter-in-law, Tim and Julyan Reid, began research for their book *Student Power and the Canadian Campus*, they quickly realized that Escott was at the forefront of developing strategies for dealing with students without causing protests to escalate into riots.

Ironically, at Glendon Reid's success only made things worse. Rather than protesting a lack of consultation, students were instead forced to rebel against the very structure of the college and university system. Having obtained a place on Glendon's committees, they often resigned in protest because the committees were simply perpetuating the problems of the system rather than addressing "the underlying political and cultural changes" required for true reform.[67] This foreshadowed a new stage of student protest – one that was increasingly coupled with a rampant drug culture that made Reid feel that he was too old to really understand the new students.[68]

When Reid retired in December 1969, in keeping with his determination to leave the College at age sixty-five, he left an uncertain legacy behind him. His relationship with York University had been tense. Ross, for example, clearly found working with Reid difficult and frustrating, "a chore that many in central administration found required great tact and patience."[69] And yet Reid was perhaps the right man for the job of creating a new institution. While he often clashed with faculty, he was clearly sympathetic and helpful. "He had style and a lot of courage," recalled one faculty member. "He was willing to try this experiment of a bilingual liberal arts college. When faculty came up to him with a new idea, saying, 'Maybe we should try this,' he would say, 'Maybe we should.'"[70]

More important, Reid was single-minded and passionate in pursuit of his guiding vision of Glendon as a fully bilingual, fully residential, liberal arts college. Admittedly, the Glendon College he left in 1969 was not the one he had set out to build five years earlier. A persistent lack of funding, opposition to compulsory courses in English and French, and a rapidly changing university culture made sure of that. Still, the College had not only survived its first four turbulent years but also maintained much of its bilingual character and its focus on Canadian public affairs and civic life. Though Reid's insistence on bilingualism and his popular image as a diplomat sometimes combined to give the College a stuffy reputation as a school for civil servants and to limit enrollment, Reid was justifiably proud of his efforts to make Glendon a bilingual institution long before the concept was popular elsewhere in Canada.[71] Even today, the political science mini-calendar reflects Reid's hope that Glendon graduates would go on "to make creative contributions to the public life of the Canadian state."[72] And today Glendon continues to be a small, liberal arts, bilingual college.

NOTES

1 "A Summary of the History of Glendon College," J.A. Becker, 28 August 1968, Glendon College Papers, 1974-020/019 (471), York University Archives (YA); and "Resolutions Concerning Glendon College Passed by York University Senate," 30 September 1965, Glendon College Papers, 1974-020/002 (05), YA.

2 Martin Friedland, *The University of Toronto: A History* (Toronto: University of Toronto Press, 2002), 340, 353.

3 Escott Reid to Timothy E. Reid, 5 August 1964, Escott Reid Papers Volume 39 File: Correspondence, 1 of 2, 1964–1965, National Archives of Canada (NAC).

4 Tim Reid to Escott Reid, August 1964, Escott Reid Papers, Volume 39 File: Correspondence, 1 of 2, 1964–1965, NAC.

5 Norman Mackenzie to Escott Reid, *ca* August 1964, Escott Reid Papers, Volume 39, File: Correspondence, 1 of 2, 1964–1965, NAC.

6 Escott Reid, "Memorandum on Discussion with L.B. Pearson, 27 August 1964," Escott Reid Papers, Volume 35, File 31, NAC.

7 Escott Reid to L.B. Pearson, September 1964, Escott Reid Papers, Volume 35, File: Pearson, L.B., NAC.

8 Notes from 18 August 1964, visit to Glendon College; Murray Ross to Escott Reid, 11 September 1964; W.W. Small to Escott Reid, 17 December 1964, Escott Reid Papers, Volume 39 File: Correspondence, 1 of 2, 1964–1965, NAC.

9 Escott Reid to W. Small, 11 May 1965, Escott Reid Papers, Volume 39 File: Correspondence, 2 of 2, 1964–1965, NAC.

10 Frank Underhill to Escott Reid, 5 February 1965, Escott Reid Papers, Volume 39 File: Correspondence, 1 of 2, 1964–1965, NAC.

11 Escott Reid to Murray Ross, 4 January 1965, Escott Reid Papers, Volume 39 File: Correspondence, 1 of 2, 1964–1965, NAC. For further discussion on the nature of student residences, see Alyson E. King, "Centres of 'Home-like Influence': Residences for Women at the University of Toronto," *Material History Review* 49 (Spring 1999) 39–59.

12 Frank Underhill to Escott Reid, 5 February 1965, Escott Reid Papers, Volume 39 File: Correspondence, 1 of 2, 1964–1965, NAC.

13 Ibid.

14 Frank Underhill to Escott Reid, 13 February 1965, Escott Reid Papers, Volume 39, File: Correspondence, 1 of 2, 1964–1965, NAC.

15 Norman Mackenzie to Escott Reid, 18 January 1965, and 3 February 1965, Escott Reid Papers, Volume 39 File: Correspondence, 1 of 2, 1964–1965, NAC.

16 "Memorandum for the Principal-Designate," 8 March 1965, Glendon College Papers, 1974-020/019 (471), YA.

17 Copy of Senate Minutes, 24 June 1965, Glendon College Papers, 1974-020/019 (471), YA.

18 Murray Ross to Escott Reid, 28 June 1965, Escott Reid Papers, Volume 39 File: Correspondence, 2 of 2, 1964–1965, NAC.

19 Escott Reid to Murray Ross, 12 July 1965, Escott Reid Papers, Volume 39 File: Correspondence, 2 of 2, 1964–1965, NAC.

20 Escott Reid, *Radical Mandarin: The Memoirs of Escott Reid* (Toronto: University of Toronto Press, 1989), 347.

21 Interview with John T. Saywell, 4 February 2003.

22 Escott Reid to Murray Ross, 15 July 1965, Escott Reid Papers, Volume 39 File: Correspondence, 2 of 2, 1964–1965, NAC.

23 Interview with John T. Saywell, 4 February 2003.

24 Escott Reid to John Holmes, 15 July 1965, Correspondence File: Escott Reid, John Holmes Papers, Canadian Institute of International Affairs (CIIA).

25 Escott Reid to Murray Ross, 21 September 1965, Escott Reid Papers, Volume 38 File: Correspondence, 1 of 5, 1965–1969, NAC. Reid notes in his memoirs

that in June 1965 he told Ross that he would be unwilling to take up his position if the Senate insisted on having the curriculum for the first two years at Glendon identical to that of York (*Radical Mandarin*, 345).

26 Escott Reid to Murray Ross, 23 March 1966, Escott Reid Papers, Volume 39 File: Correspondence, Reports and Speeches, 1 of 5, 1966–1967, NAC.

27 Murray Ross to Escott Reid, 3 May 1967, Escott Reid Papers, Correspondence, Reports and Speeches, 1 of 5, 1966–67, NAC.

28 Escott Reid to Murray Ross, 29 May 1968, Glendon College Papers, 1974-020/001 (1), YA.

29 Series of letters dated 9 October 1968, 1 November 1968, 5 November 1968, and 19 November 1968, Glendon College Papers, 1974-020/019 (471), YA.

30 Escott Reid to The President, 4 December 1968, 1974-020/019 (471), YA.

31 Escott Reid to Murray Ross, 26 May 1969, Escott Reid Papers, Volume 39 File: Selected Correspondence 5 of 5 1965–1969, and Escott Reid to Dr. Robert C. Rae, Research Associate, Office of the President, 14 April 1969, Escott Reid Papers, Volume 40 File: Correspondence, Reports and Speeches 2 of 5 1969, NAC. Reid was assisted in the production of the report by Professor Michiel Horn.

32 Escott Reid to Bertrand Gerstein, People's Credit Jewellers, Toronto, 26 May 1969, Escott Reid Papers, Volume 39 File: Selected Correspondence 5 of 5 1965–69, NAC.

33 Conversation with Michiel Horn, 24 September 2001. In his memoirs, Reid notes a comment by Nollaig MacKenzie who described the atmosphere as one of crisis. See *Radical Mandarin*, 343.

34 John T. Saywell to Murray Ross, 17 June 1968, Glendon College Papers, 1974-020/001 (1), YA.

35 Escott Reid to Murray Ross, 1 May 1968, Escott Reid Papers, Volume 39 File: Selected Correspondence 3 of 5, 1965–69, NAC.

36 Escott Reid to Dean H. Harris, 6 March 1969, and Minutes of a Meeting of the Executive Committee of the Glendon College Faculty Council, 10 March 1969, Glendon College Papers, 1974-020/020 (477), YA.

37 Murray G. Ross to Escott Reid, 10 March 1969, Glendon College Papers, 1974-020/020 (477), YA.

38 Extract from the Minutes of the Meeting of the Board of Governors, York University, 10 March 1969, Glendon College Papers, 1974-020/020 (477), YA.

39 "Terry," Bishop's University, to Escott Reid, 21 April 1965, Escott Reid Papers, Volume 39 File: Correspondence, 1 of 2, 1964–65, NAC.

40 Escott Reid to Dean Harris, 17 October 1968, Glendon College Papers, 1974-020/001(02), YA.

41 Ibid.

42 "Faculty council cuts compulsory English," newspaper clipping, 24 October 1968, Glendon College Papers, 1974-020/001(08), YA.

43 Escott Reid to Dean Harris, 4 November 1968, Escott Reid Papers, Volume 39, File: Selected Correspondence 4 of 5, 1965–69, NAC.

44 For more on student activism in Canada in the 1960s, see Cyril Levitt, "Canada," in Philip G. Altbach, ed., *Student Political Activism: An International Reference Handbook* (New York: Greenwood Press, 1989), 419–26; Cyril Levitt, *Children of Privilege: Student Revolt in the Sixties: A Study of Student Movements in Canada, the United States, and West Germany* (Toronto: University of Toronto Press, 1984).

45 "Comment," *Pro Tem*, 12 November 1965, Escott Reid Papers, Volume 42, Scrapbook, Volume 3, 1965–66, NAC.

46 "Comment," *Pro Tem*, 12 November 1965, Escott Reid Papers, Volume 42, Scrapbook, Volume 3, 1965–66, NAC; "Students knock principal," *Toronto Star* clipping, 16 November 1965, Escott Reid Papers, Volume 42, Scrapbook, Volume 3, 1965–66, NAC; "Rift healed, principal host to students," *Globe and Mail*, 28 December 1965, Escott Reid Papers, Volume 42, Scrapbook, Volume 3, 1965–66, NAC.

47 "The Idea of Glendon College," 13 January 1966, Glendon College papers, 1974-020/002(05), YA.

48 Warren Gerard, "York: University of Change," *Globe and Mail*, 16 September 1966, Escott Reid Papers, Volume 42, Scrapbook, Volume 3, 1965–66, NAC.

49 "Opinion Two," *Pro Tem* 21 January 1966, Escott Reid Papers, Volume 42, Scrapbook, Volume 3, 1965–66, NAC.

50 Escott Reid to Norman Smith, 29 March 1961, Escott Reid Papers, Volume 36, NAC.

51 Interviews with Richard J. Schultz, 14 January 2003, and Timothy Reid, 14 January 2003.

52 "York students demand more money as Pearson opens Glendon," *Toronto Star*, 1 October 1966, Escott Reid Papers, Volume 42, Scrapbook, Volume 3, 1965–66, NAC.

53 "Students picket Pearson at college opening," *Globe and Mail*, 1 October 1966, Escott Reid Papers, Volume 42, Scrapbook, Volume 3, 1965–66, NAC.

54 "Responsibility and Revolt, The Principal's Opening Address to New Students," Escott Reid, 18 September 1967, 5, Glendon College Papers, 1974-020/001 (1), YA. See also Reid's speech to students at Ridley College, "A Student Generation in Revolt," 8 June 1968, Glendon College Papers, 1974-020/017 (8), YA.

55 "Responsibility and Revolt," 5.

56 Escott Reid, "A Student Generation in Revolt," speech to Ridley College, Toronto, 8 June 1968, Glendon College Papers, 1974-020/017 (8), YA.

57 Jim Park, Student Council, to students and faculty members of Glendon College, 26 August 1968, Escott Reid Papers, Volume 39, Correspondence, Reports and Speeches, 3 of 6, 1968, NAC.

58 Ibid, 2.

59 Ibid, 2; Undated brochure, Glendon College Papers, 1974-020/022 (523), YA.

60 "A University is for the People," undated, *ca* September 1968, 4, Glendon College Papers, 1974-020/002 (07), YA.

61 Ibid.

62 Dean H.S. Harris to All Members of the Glendon College Faculty, 4 September 1968, Glendon College Papers, 1974-020/001 (02), YA.

63 "A University is for the People," undated, *ca* September 1968, Glendon College Papers, 1974-020/002 (07), YA.

64 Those making use of the head table had always paid extra for the privilege of having table service.

65 Series of letters to Jim Park of the Student Council dated 16 September 1968, Glendon College Papers, 1974-020/007 (63), YA and Escott Reid Papers, Volume 39, File: Selected Correspondence 4 of 5, 1965–69, NAC.

66 "Frosh register, foil Glendon plan," *Excalibur*, 19 September 1968, Escott Reid Papers, MG31 E46 Volume 44, Scrapbook, Volume 5, Sept. 1968–October 1969, NAC.

67 Minutes of the Faculty Council, 26 March 1969, Escott Reid Papers, Volume 40, File: Correspondence, Reports and Speeches, 2 of 5, NAC.

68 Interviews with Richard J. Schultz 14 January 2003, and Timothy Reid 14 January 2003. Tim and Julyan Reid, eds, *Student Power and the Canadian Campus* (Toronto: Peter Martin Associates, 1969).

69 Murray Ross, *The Way Must Be Tried: The Memoirs of a University Man* (Toronto: University of Toronto Press, 1992), 126.

70 Professor Tursman, quoted in newspaper clipping, "Glendon: Plus ça change ..." *ca* 1986, Escott Reid Papers, Volume 39, Correspondence, Reports and Speeches, 5 of 5, 1969, NAC.

71 Reid, *Radical Mandarin*, 343.

72 Political Science Minicalendar, 2000–2001 (accessed October 2, 2001) http://gl.yorku.ca:8008/acad_polsci.nsf/main_page?OpenPage.

Conclusion

STÉPHANE ROUSSEL AND GREG DONAGHY

In retirement, Escott Reid remained an active commentator on international relations, Canadian diplomacy, and public policy. Indeed, from the relative seclusion of his beloved farm at Ste Cécile de Masham, he emerged in the 1970s and 1980s as a formidable memorist, documenting in exquisite detail his own farsightedness and the shortcomings of his contemporaries – friend and foe alike. In his first book, *Time of Fear and Hope: The Making of the North Atlantic Treaty*, Reid poses as the high-minded visionary, whose efforts to create the nucleus for a trans-Atlantic federation were betrayed and sold short by Canada's slightly nefarious ambassador to the United States, Hume Wrong.[1] In his subsequent books he is no less blunt, vigorously rewaging lost battles over the language of the UN Charter or the wisdom of American military aid to Pakistan.[2]

Though these works often provided much raw material and plenty of inspiration for historians and students, they helped to stereotype Reid as a frustrated idealist who doggedly pursued his distant objectives with little regard for the possible. At the same time, Reid's participant-memoirs reinforced the tendency of Canadian scholars to celebrate the 1940s and 1950s as the "golden age" in Canadian diplomacy, when the struggle for national advantage took backseat to a more noble search for a new world order. This small collection of essays on Reid and his evolving role as diplomat, international civil servant, and academic tries to understand Reid on his own terms, using the documentary record to explore his idealism, its limits, and how he sought to transform his rhetoric into action. And by extension, the collection tries to cast some new light on the nature of post-war Canadian diplomacy.

There is little doubt, as virtually every contributor here readily acknowledges, that Reid's defining characteristic was his progressive idealism. Whether battling against an insular complacency at the Canadian Institute of International Affairs during the 1930s or struggling to craft a "people's charter" for the United Nations in the mid-1940s, Reid was at his dynamic best when he pressed against the established order. His colleagues, particularly his longtime friend and mentor L.B. Pearson, admired his capacity for hard work and his far-sighted intellectual vision.

But Reid's foresight came with a price. His judgment, which often reflected the unyielding self-righteousness and arrogance of the crusader, was frequently questioned and found lacking. His idealism and the passion that accompanied it undermined many of his most treasured initiatives. In the catholicity of his enthusiasms, Reid was often unable to distinguish the vital from the unimportant, frittering away his time and energies for little return. Engaging his foes on several fronts at once, Reid was liable to exhaust himself and alienate his colleagues, especially the arch-realist Wrong, with whom he clashed repeatedly over the UN and NATO. Reid's recurring struggles with depression and exhaustion – at the UN in 1945, during the darkest days of the Korean War in 1950–51, and at the height of the Suez Crisis in 1956 – rendered his judgment increasingly suspect and ultimately prevented him from reaching the highest posts in Canada's foreign service.

However, the detailed case studies in this book reveal a side of Reid that is too often neglected and overlooked. This Reid was conscious of his demons, learned from his encounters with them, and constantly struggled against them. This Reid was the skilful, hard-working diplomat whose memoranda and despatches, however passionate, were also carefully reasoned and tightly argued treatises on Canada's national interest. They give contemporary readers pause and suggest a continuing need to develop a more nuanced understanding of the forces animating their country's foreign policy in the two decades after the Second World War. As Mackenzie makes clear in his study of Reid at the UN, Canada and its diplomats, Reid included, were interested less in a perfect world organization than in ensuring that Canada's rights and interests were fully acknowledged and protected. Reid, argue Roussel and Haglund, demonstrated a similarly realistic appreciation of where Canada's interests lay during the negotiations that led to the North Atlantic Treaty in 1949. Indeed, in their view, it is Reid's *realpolitik*, not his idealism, that is his lasting contribution to the discussion of Canadian foreign policy. And perhaps they are right, for even in post-colonial India, where the scope for his idealistic vision was unparalleled, Reid rarely lost sight of his ultimate objective: to enhance relations between New Delhi and Ottawa in order to promote Canada's national interest.

Reid remains relevant today. Perhaps more than ever before, in the aftermath of the Cold War and the September 2001 terrorist attacks on New York and Washington, Canada's international environment is dominated by the preoccupations of one great power – the United States. Again, Ottawa is forced to wrestle with and define Canada's role in North American defence, contemplating, as Reid did from 1940 to 1947, the prospect of a terribly unequal partnership. Though anxious to demonstrate their solidarity with Washington for a host of good and practical reasons, Canadians must be careful lest too close a partnership jeopardize crucial elements of their national identity, if not their very sovereignty. Like Reid sixty years ago, many will reach almost instinctively for a counterweight metaphor[3]; it is doubtful whether their efforts will prove any more effective than Reid's.

Canadian policy-makers might seek a more promising solution to their security dilemma by recasting the problem in terms to which Reid would surely subscribe. On this longer view, American success in the war against terrorism depends as much on the creation of a more stable and just international order as on military force. To diminish the hatred of its foes and to woo its allies, Washington must begin to address the unfulfilled promise of the United Nations and the cries of most of its members for genuine social and economic progress. From this perspective, Reid's vision of a people's UN, of a democratic Asia joined to the West, and of a real North Atlantic community emerging from NATO seem increasingly necessary and realistic.[4] Perhaps our initially pragmatic response to the American challenge since September 2001 ought to be accompanied by a forceful idealism that might lead us toward a less dramatic but more enduring solution.

NOTES

1 Escott Reid, *Time of Fear and Hope: The Making of the North Atlantic Treaty, 1947–1949* (Toronto: McClelland and Stewart, 1977), chapter 19.

2 Escott Reid, *Envoy to Nehru* (Toronto: Oxford University Press, 1981), 99–116; See also Escott Reid, *On Duty: A Canadian at the Making of the United Nations, 1945–1949* (Toronto: McClelland and Stewart, 1983), 66–8.

3 For a recent evocation of the counterweight, see Roy MacLaren, "Wanted: EU Trading Partners: It's perilous for Canada to put all its eggs in one U.S. basket," *Globe and Mail*, 16 August 2002.

4 In certain respects, NATO has already begun to resemble the North Atlantic community that Reid envisioned in 1948. On this point see Stéphane Roussel, "L'instant kantien: la contribution canadienne à la création de la communauté nord-atlantique," in Greg Donaghy, ed., *Canada and the Early Cold War, 1943–1957* (Ottawa: Department of Foreign Affairs and International Trade, 1999), 119–56. See also Thomas Risse-Kappen, *Cooperation among Democracies. The European Influence on U.S. Foreign Policy* (Princeton, N.J.: Princeton University Press, 1995).

Bibliography

Primary Sources

BISHOP'S UNIVERSITY ARCHIVES
T.W.L. MacDermot Papers

CANADIAN INSTITUTE OF INTERNATIONAL AFFAIRS
J.W. Holmes Papers

NATIONAL ARCHIVES OF CANADA
Department of External Affairs Records
Escott Reid Papers
F.H. Underhill Papers
L.B. Pearson Papers
W.L.M. King Papers

QUEEN'S UNIVERSITY ARCHIVES
Grant Dexter Papers

REID PAPERS (STE CECILE DE MASHAM)

SCOTTISH RECORD OFFICE
Lord Lothian Papers

SOUTH AFRICAN ARCHIVES
Charles te Waters Papers

UNITED STATES NATIONAL ARCHIVES
State Department Records

UNIVERSITY OF BRITISH COLUMBIA ARCHIVES
N.A.M. MacKenzie Papers

WORLD BANK ARCHIVES

YORK UNIVERSITY ARCHIVES
Glendon College Papers

Books and Articles

Barry, Donald, ed. *Documents on Canadian External Relations, Volume 18:
1952.* Ottawa: Minister of Supply and Services Canada, 1990.
– ed. *Documents on Canadian External Relations, Volume 19: 1953.* Ottawa:
Minister of Supply and Services Canada, 1991.
Bell, George. "Whither Canada? Long Term Strategic Requirements." In Alex
Morrison, ed., *A Continuing Commitment: Canada and North Atlantic Secu-
rity.* Toronto, Canadian Institute for Strategic Studies, 1992, 43–52.
Beauregard, Claude. "La coopération militaire et les relations canado-améri-
caines vues par un groupe d'éminents canadiens en 1940," *Revue canadienne
de défense* 21 (Summer 1992), 33–6.
Bhagwati, Jagdish. *India in Transition: Freeing the Economy.* Oxford: Clarendon
Press, 1993.
Bothwell, Robert. "Eyes West: Canada and the Cold War in Asia." In Greg Don-
aghy, ed., *Canada and the Early Cold War, 1943–1957.* Ottawa: Department
of Foreign Affairs and International Trade, 1998, 59–70.
Brebner, J. Bartlet. *North Atlantic Triangle: The Interplay of Canada, the United
States and Great Britain.* Toronto: McClelland and Stewart, 1945.
– "A Changing North Atlantic Triangle," *International Journal* 3 (Fall 1948),
309–19.
Buteux, Paul. "Commitment or Retreat: Redefining the Canadian Role in the
Alliance," *Canadian Defence Quarterly* 23 (December 1993), 12–16.
Canada, Department of External Affairs. *Conference Series, 1945, No. 2, Report
on the United Nations Conference on International Organization Held at San
Francisco, 25th April – 26th June, 1945.* Ottawa: King's Printer, 1945.

Canada, Department of External Affairs. *Conference Series, 1946, No. 1, Report on the First Part of the First Session of the General Assembly of the United Nations Held in London, January 10 – February 14, 1946.* Ottawa: King's Printer, 1946.

Canada. *Treaty Series,* 1942.

Canada. Secretary of State for External Affairs. *Foreign Policy for Canadians. Europe.* Ottawa: Information Canada, 1970.

Canada, House of Commons, Standing Committee on National Defence and Veterans Affairs. Minutes of Proceedings and Evidence, 1991.

Dittmer, Lowell. "Political Culture and Political Symbolism," *World Politics* 29 (July 1977), 552–83.

Donaghy, Greg. "Pacific Diplomacy: Canadian Statecraft and the Korean War, 1950–53." In Rick Guisso and Yong-Sik Yoo, eds, *Canada and Korea: Perspectives 2000.* Toronto: University of Toronto Press and the Centre for Korean Studies, 2001, 80–96.

– "Nehru's Reactor: The Origins of Indo-Canadian Nuclear Cooperation, 1955–59." Paper prepared for the South Asian Studies Conference, Université Laval, Québec City, 25–27 May 2001.

– ed.. *Documents on Canadian External Relations, Volume 20: 1954.* Ottawa: Canada Communication Group, 1997.

Donneur, André P.. "La fin de la guerre froide: le Canada et la sécurité européenne," *Études internationales* 23 (March 1992), 121–38.

Eayrs, James. *In Defence of Canada: Peacemaking and Deterrence.* Toronto: University of Toronto Press, 1972.

English, John, and Norman Hillmer. "Canada's Alliances," *Revue internationale d'histoire militaire* 54 (1982), 31–52.

Epp, Roger. "On Justifying the Alliance: Canada, NATO and World Order." In Michael K. Hawes and Joel J. Sokolsky, eds, *North American Perspectives on European Security.* New York: Edwin Mellen, 1990, 89–121.

Evatt, Herbert Vere. *The United Nations.* Cambridge, Mass.: Harvard University Press, 1948.

Gopal, S. "The Halycon Fifties," *The Book Review* (India) July–August 1981.

Granatstein, J.L. "The Conservative Party and the Ogdensburg Agreement," *International Journal* 22 (Winter 1966–67), 73–6.

– *A Man of Influence: Norman A. Robertson and Canadian Statecraft, 1929–68.* Toronto: Deneau, 1981.

– *The Ottawa Men: The Civil Service Mandarins, 1935–1957.* Toronto: Oxford University Press, 1982.

– and Robert Bothwell. "'A Self-Evident National Duty': Canadian Foreign Policy, 1935–1939," *Journal of Imperial and Commonwealth History* 3 (January 1975), 212–33.

Gray, Colin S. "Strategic Culture as Context: The First Generation of Theory Strikes Back," *Review of International Studies* 25 (January 1999), 49–69.

Haglund, David G. *The North Atlantic Triangle Revisited: Canadian Grand Strategy at Century's End*. Toronto: Canadian Institue of International Affairs, 2000.

Halstead, John. "Future Directions for the Alliance," *The Atlantic Council Letter* 3 (July 1992), 2.

Hasluck, Paul. *Diplomatic Witness: Australian Foreign Affairs 1941–1947*. Melbourne: Melbourne University Press, 1980.

Hilliker, John F. *Canada's Department of External Affairs: Volume 1: Coming of Age, 1909–1945*. Montreal and Kingston: McGill-Queen's University Press, 1990.

– ed. *Documents on Canadian External Relations, Volume 9, 1942–43*. Ottawa: Supply and Services Canada, 1980.

– ed. *Documents on Canadian External Relations, Volume 11, 1944–1945, Part II*. Ottawa: Supply and Services Canada, 1990.

Hillmer, Norman, and Donald Page, eds, *Documents on Canadian External Relations, Volume 13: 1947*. Ottawa: Canada Communication Group, 1993.

Holmes, John W. *The Shaping of Peace: Canada and the Search for World Order, 1943–1957*. 2 vols. Toronto: University of Toronto Press, 1979.

Horn, Michiel. *The League for Social Reconstruction: Intellectual Origins of the Democratic Left in Canada, 1930–42*. Toronto: University of Toronto Press, 1980.

Jockel, Joseph T. *No Boundaries Upstairs: Canada, the United States, and the Origins of North American Air Defence, 1945–1958*. Vancouver: University of British Columbia Press, 1987.

Johnston, Alastair Iain, "Thinking about Strategic Culture," *International Security* 19 (Spring 1995), 32–64.

Kapur, Devesh, John P. Lewis, and Richard Webb. *The World Bank: Its First Half Century, Volume 1: History*. Washington, D.C.: Brookings Institute Press, 1997.

Keating, Tom. *Canada and World Order: The Multilateralist Tradition in Canadian Foreign Policy*. Toronto: McClelland and Stewart, 1993.

– and Larry Pratt. *Canada, NATO and the Bomb: The Western Alliance in Crisis*. Edmonton: Hurtig, 1988.

Keeble, Edna. "Rethinking the 1971 White Paper and Trudeau's Impact on Canadian Foreign Policy," *The American Review of Canadian Studies* 27 (Winter 1997), 545–69.

Kennan, George ("X"). "The Sources of Soviet Conduct," *Foreign Affairs* 25 (July 1947), 566–82.

King, Alyson E. "Centres of 'Home-like Influence': Residences for Women at the University of Toronto," *Material History Review* 49 (Spring 1999), 39–59.

Kurth, James. "Inside the Cave: The Banality of I.R. Studies," *National Interest* 53 (Fall 1998), 34–45.

Legault, Albert. "Trente ans de politique de défense canadienne." In Paul Painchaud, ed., *Le Canada et le Québec sur la scène internationale*. Québec: Presses de l'Université Laval – Centre québécois de relations internationales, 1977, 149–77.

Legro, Jeffrey W., and Andrew Moravcsik. "Is Anybody Still a Realist?," *International Security* 24 (Fall 1999), 5–55.

Lenarcic, David. "Bordering on War: A Comparison of Canadian and American Neutralist Sentiment during the 1930s," *American Review of Canadian Studies* (Summer 1994), 217–28.

– "Pragmatism over Principle: The Canadian Neutrality League," *Journal of Canadian Studies* 29 (Summer 1994), 128–46.

– *Canada's Frontier Is on the Maginot Line: Some Canadian Views on the European Balance of Power and the Fall of France*. unpub. MS.

Létourneau, Paul. "Les motivations originales du Canada lors de la création de l'OTAN (1948–1950)." In Paul Létourneau, ed., *Le Canada et l'OTAN après 40 ans, 1949–1989*. Québec: Centre québécois de relations internationales, 1992, 49–66.

– "Comment limiter un marché léonin? Le Canada et le couplage stratégique avec l'Europe (1943–1952)." *XVII Congresso Internazionale di Storia Militare*. Rome: Commission internationale d'histoire militaire, 1993, 421–32.

Levitt, Cyril, "Canada." In Philip G. Altbach, ed., *Student Political Activism: An International Reference Handbook*. New York: Greenwood Press, Inc., 1989, 419–26.

– *Children of Privilege: Student Revolt in the Sixties: A Study of Student Movements in Canada, the United States, and West Germany*. Toronto: University of Toronto Press, 1984.

Leyton-Brown, David. "Managing Canada-United States Relations in the Context of Multilateral Alliances." In Lauren McKinsey and Kim Richard Nossal, eds, *America's Alliances and Canadian-American Relations*. Toronto: Summerhill Press, 1988, 162–79.

Lyon, Peyton V., and David Leyton-Brown. "Image and Policy Preference: Canadian Élite Views on Relations with the United States," *International Journal* 32 (Summer 1977), 640–71.

MacKenzie, David. *Canada and International Civil Aviation, 1932–1948*. Toronto: University of Toronto Press, 1989.

Mackenzie, Hector, ed. *Documents on Canadian External Relations, Volume 14: 1948*. Ottawa, Canada Communication Group, 1994.

– "Canada, the Cold War and the Negotiation of the North Atlantic Treaty." In John Hilliker and Mary Halloran, eds, *Diplomatic Documents and Their Users*. Ottawa: Department of Foreign Affairs and International Trade, 1995, 145–73.

– "Myth and Reality of Canada's 'Internationalism' – from the League of Nations to the United Nations." Public Lecture, Carleton University, 3 November 2001.

McKercher, B. J. C., and Lawrence Aronsen. "Introduction," *The North Atlantic Triangle in a Changing World: Anglo-American-Canadian Relations, 1902–1956*. Toronto: University of Toronto Press, 1996, 3–11.

Morton, Desmond. "Defending the Indefensible: Some Historical Perspectives on Canadian Defence 1867–1967," *International Journal* 42 (Autumn 1987), 627–44.

Murray, David R., ed. *Documents on Canadian External Relations, Volume 7: 1939–1941 Part I*. Ottawa: Information Canada, 1974.

Nossal, Kim R. *The Politics of Canadian Foreign Policy*. Scarborough: Prentice-Hall, 1997.

Ørvik, Nils. "Canadian Security and 'Defence Against Help'," *Survival* 42 (January–February 1984), 26–31.

Osgood, Robert E. *Ideals and Self-Interest in America's Foreign Relations: The Great Transformation of the Twentieth Century*. Chicago: University of Chicago Press, Phoenix Books, 1964.

Page, Donald M., ed. *Documents on Canadian External Relations, Volume 12: 1946*. Ottawa: Supply and Services Canada, 1977.

Pearson, Geoffrey A.H. *Seize the Day: Lester B. Pearson and Crisis Diplomacy*. Ottawa: Carleton University Press, 1993.

– "Remembering Escott Reid," *Behind the Headlines* 57 (Autumn 1999), 23.

Pearson, Lester B. *Mike: The Memoirs of the Right Honourable Lester B. Pearson*. 3 vols. Toronto: University of Toronto Press, 1972–75.

– *Words and Occasions*. Toronto: University of Toronto Press, 1970.

Pentland, Charles. "L'option européenne du Canada dans les années '80," *Études internationales* 14 (March 1983), 39–58.

Perras, Galen Roger. *Franklin Roosevelt and the Origins of the Canadian-American Security Alliance, 1933–1945*. Westport: Praeger, 1998.

Pickersgill, J.W., and D.F. Forster, eds. *The Mackenzie King Record, Volume 2: 1944–1945*. Toronto: University of Toronto Press, 1968.

– eds. *The Mackenzie King Record, Volume 3: 1945–46*. Toronto: University of Toronto Press, 1970.

Plumptre, A.F.W. *Three Decades of Decision: Canada and the World Monetary System, 1944–75*. Toronto: McClelland and Stewart, 1977.

Reid, Escott [anonymous]. "Free World Recommends a Charter For the United Nations," *Free World* (May 1945), 77–83.

- "Canadian Political Parties: A Study of the Economic and Racial Bases of Conservatism and Liberalism in 1930," *Contributions to Canadian Economics* VI (1933), 7–39.
- "Can Canada Remain Neutral?," *Dalhousie Review*, XV (1935), 135–48
- "Canada and This Next War," *Canadian Forum* XIV (March 1934), 207–9.
- *Canada and the League*, MS, 1934.
- "Did Canada Cause War?," *Saturday Night* 50 (28 September 1935), 1, 3.
- "International Sanctions and World Peace," *University of Toronto Quarterly* 4 (1935), 408–17.
- "League Must Give Justice as Well as Peace," *Saturday Night* 50 (5 October 1935), 2.
- "Mr. Mackenzie King's Foreign Policy, 1935–1936," *Canadian Journal of Economics and Political Science* 3 (February 1937), 86–97.
- "The Saskatchewan Liberal Machine before 1929," *Canadian Journal of Economics and Political Science* 2 (February 1936), 27–40.
- "Canada's Role in the United Nations." In Eugene A. Forsey, ed., *Canada in a New World: Addresses given at the Canadian Institute of Public Affairs.* Toronto: Ryerson Press, 1948, 29–42.
- "The Birth of the North Atlantic Alliance," *International Journal* 22 (Summer 1967), 426–40.
- *Time of Fear and Hope: The Making of the North Atlantic Treaty, 1947–1949.* Toronto: McClelland and Stewart, 1977.
- *Envoy to Nehru.* Delhi: Oxford University Press, 1981.
- *On Duty: A Canadian at the Making of the United Nations, 1945–1949.* Toronto: McClelland and Stewart, 1983.
- "The Art of the Almost Impossible: Unwavering Canadian Support for the Emerging Atlantic Alliance." In André de Staerke, ed., *NATO's Anxious Birth: The Prophetic Vision of the 1940s.* New York: St Martin's Press, 1985, 76–86.
- *Hungary and Suez 1956: A View from New Delhi.* Oakville: Mosaic Press, 1986.
- "The Creation of the North Atlantic Alliance." In J.L. Granatstein, ed., *Canadian Foreign Policy: Historical Readings.* Toronto: Copp Clark Pitman, 1986, 158–82.
- *Radical Mandarin: The Memoirs of Escott Reid.* Toronto: University of Toronto Press, 1989.
Rempel, Roy. *Counterweights. The Failure of Canada's German and European Policy (1955–1995).* Montreal and Kingston: McGill-Queen's University Press, 1996.

Ritchie, Charles. *Diplomatic Passport: More Undiplomatic Diaries, 1946–1962*. Toronto: Macmillan, 1981.

– *The Siren Years: A Canadian Diplomat Abroad 1937–1945*. Toronto: Macmillan, 1974.

Robertson, Gordon. *Memoirs of a Very Civil Servant: Mackenzie King to Pierre Trudeau*. Toronto: University of Toronto Press, 2000.

Rogers, Benjamin, et al. "Escott Reid: Issues and Causes," *Behind the Headlines* 50 (Autumn 1992).

Rose, Gideon. "Neoclassical Realism and Theories of Foreign Policy," *World Politics* 51 (October 1998), 144–72.

Roussel, Stéphane. "Amère Amérique ... L'OTAN et l'intérêt national du Canada," *Revue canadienne de défense* 22 (February 1993), 35–42.

– Paul Létourneau, and Roch Legault. "Le Canada et la sécurité européenne (1943–1952): À la recherche de l'équilibre des puissances," *Revue canadienne de défense* 23 (Summer 1994), 23–7; 24 (Fall 1994), 17–22.

– "L'instant kantien: la contribution canadienne à la création de la communauté nord-atlantique." In Greg Donaghy, ed., *Canada and the Early Cold War, 1943-1957*. Ottawa: Department of Foreign Affairs and International Trade, 1999, 119–56.

Smith, Denis. *Diplomacy of Fear: Canada and the Cold War 1941–1948*. Toronto: University of Toronto Press, 1988.

Sokolsky, Joel J. "A Seat at the Table: Canada and Its Alliances." In B.D. Hunt and R.G. Haycock, eds, *Canada's Defence: Perspectives on Policy in the Twentieth Century*. Toronto: Copp Clark Pitman, 1993, 147–62.

Soward, F.H. *Canada in World Affairs, From Normandy to Paris, 1944–1946*. Toronto: Oxford University Press, 1950.

Stacey, C.P. *Canada and the Age of Conflict: A History of Canadian External Policies, Volume 2: 1921–1948, The Mackenzie King Era*. Toronto: University of Toronto Press, 1981.

Stairs, Denis. "Realists at Work: Canadian Policy Makers and the Politics of Transition from Hot War to Cold War." In Greg Donaghy, ed., *Canada and the Early Cold War, 1943–1957*. Ottawa: Department of Foreign Affairs and International Trade, 1999, 91–116.

Tarr, Edgar. "Canada in World Affairs," *International Affairs* 16 (September 1937).

Tucker, Michael J. *Canadian Foreign Policy: Contemporary Issues and Themes*. Toronto: McGraw-Hill Ryerson, 1980.

Tucker, Robert W. *The Radical Left and American Foreign Policy*. Washington Center of Foreign Policy Research: Studies in International Affairs, 15. Baltimore: Johns Hopkins Press, 1971.

Waltz, Kenneth N. *Theory of International Politics*. Reading, Mass.: Addison-Wesley, 1979.

Willoughby, William R. *The Joint Organizations of Canada and the United States*. Toronto, University of Toronto Press, 1979.

Young, Alice K. "Escott Reid as Cold Warrior?: A Canadian Diplomat's Reflections on the Soviet Union." In J.L. Black and Norman Hillmer, eds, *Nearly Neighbours: Canada and the Soviet Union: From Cold War to Détente and Beyond*. Kingston: R.P. Frye, 1989, 29–41.

Contributors

Greg Donaghy is head of the historical section at Foreign Affairs Canada.

J.L. Granatstein is a historian and former director and chief executive officer of the Canadian War Museum.

David G. Haglund is the Sir Edward Peacock Professor of Political Studies at Queen's University.

Alyson King teaches history at Trent University.

Hector Mackenzie is senior departmental historian at Foreign Affairs Canada.

Bruce Muirhead is professor of history at Lakehead University.

Stéphane Roussel holds the Canada Research Chair in Canadian Defense and Foreign Policy at the Université du Québec à Montréal.

Index

Page numbers in italic indicate a photograph. Escott Reid's name has been abbreviated to ER.